EZRA POUND

A CLOSE-UP

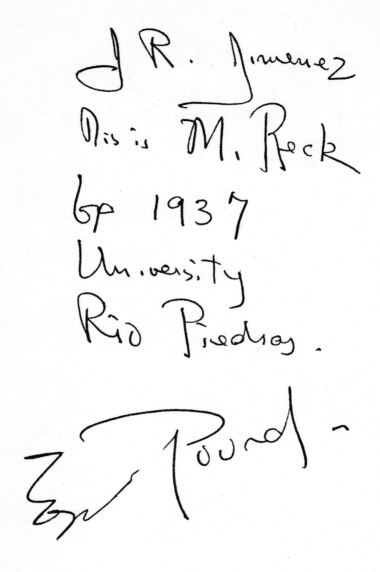

[A note introducing Michael Reck to Juan Ramón Jiménez, Nobel Laureate for Literature in 1956.]

Ezra Pound

A CLOSE-UP

by Michael Reck

McGraw-Hill Book Company

New York Toronto London Sydney

For my sons

CONTENTS

Introduction ix

PART ONE Cleansing Helicon 1
1. *Crawfordsville to Venice* 3
2. *A Yank Among the Georgians* 11
3. *Blast and After* 26
4. *70 bis rue Notre-Dame-des-Champs* 40
5. *Retirement in Rapallo* 48
6. *Rome Radio* 56

PART TWO Mr. Pound's Elizabethan Age 73
1. *Saint Elizabeth's* 75
2. *Where the Dead Walked* 78
3. *An Exile in His Own Land* 85
4. *The Man Ezra Pound* 110
5. *"What Does Mr. Pound Believe?"* 122
6. *Farewell* 132

PART THREE Back to Italy 137

PART FOUR The Meaning of Pound 151
1. *A Universal American* 153
2. *Maintain Antisepsis* 160
3. *A Genius at Work* 166
4. *Ear for the Sea Surge* 176
5. *The Elusive Mr. Pound* 182
6. *Reading the Cantos* 187
Index 197

INTRODUCTION

Reading Ezra Pound's poetry is often thought to be extraordinarily difficult. Once I heard a bright young American literature instructor at Harvard bill Achilles Fang as the *only* person who understood Pound's mind. Fang would certainly not have claimed this—and I believe the matter is not nearly so complex. Perhaps I may ease the way a bit by relating what I know of the man and his verse, and recording some Pound history as I experienced it myself.

Ezra Pound, very likely the most influential English-language writer of this century, was incarcerated at Saint Elizabeth's insane asylum in Washington, D.C., from 1946 to 1958, after being found "mentally incompetent" to stand trial for treason. I visited him there and in Italy over a period of fifteen years. I took no notes while I was seeing him because then I had no thought of turning my visits to any use except that of cultivating a friendship and acquiring knowledge. So the firsthand parts of my account are entirely from memory. However, I may even claim some merit in not depending on notes. What is written here remains after being sifted through memory's sieve, and time and forgetfulness may have brought perspective.

"Mr. Pound's Elizabethan Age" is of course his *Saint* Elizabethan Age. "Saint" refers only to the hospital—not to Ezra. My book is not a hagiography, so I shall not gloss over his singular economic ideas, about which he often spoke at Saint Elizabeth's. But Pound's political errors may be better known than his character. And that character— a very magnanimous one—is worth describing.

Though the Saint Elizabeth's years were far from the most glorious of Pound's life, they are interesting, for his re-encounter with his homeland took place under very strange conditions. The circumstances were tragic, and the protagonist had the grandeur and flaws of a tragic hero. Pound had by no means lost his poetic powers; some of the Cantos written at this time are among his finest. "The old hand as stylist still holding its cunning."

To put him into perspective, I shall also tell the tale of the poet's life as a whole. I may have a small special insight here, having often discussed past things with Pound at Saint Elizabeth's. And while I was compiling the present book, Mrs. Pound sat with me patiently to help fill gaps in my knowledge of Pound's life. This is a life so full of intellectual adventure, so distinguished for literary achievement —both in his own writings and in discovering and aiding other writers—and so strange in its denouement, that there is really nothing like it in all modern literature. Whatever one may think of Pound's politics, one can only say of the poet and the person: this was a man.

The reader will, I hope, pardon an apologetic tone that pops up here and there in the present book. This kind of whining will not be necessary fifty years hence, when people will remember Pound's achievements, *not* his politics. Consider the high reputation of Dostoievsky today, even in Soviet Russia—and that novelist was an arch-reactionary in comparison with whom Pound seems very radical or liberal indeed. I have treated Pound's politics because the issues that so concerned him are still live in our memory. But the issues will pass away. The poet will remain.

Above all, I hope to bring the reader closer to Pound's poetry. He has written that criticism should be self-consuming; it should do its work and then disappear, leaving one face to face with the poem itself. I agree. If the present book helps make Pound's poetry more alive, that is its justification. As the Zen Buddhists say, we should not confound the finger pointing at the moon with the moon itself.

　　　　. . . de su pecho
　　tan grande es el corazón
　　que teme, no sin razón,
　　que el mundo le viene estrecho.

　　So wide the heart
that feeds his marrow
it fears, not without cause,
lest the world be, for it, too narrow.

　　from Calderón

PART ONE

Cleansing Helicon

I

Crawfordsville to Venice

A biographer of Byron declares that wildfire leapt about his cradle. It is not recorded that wildfire leapt about Ezra Pound's cradle. Nevertheless . . .

From his early days, he gathered storms about himself. In the juicy cliché of one of our critical mahatmas, he was a "controversial figure."

Pound burst into the London literary salons of the early nineteen-tens like a Wild West figure. People remembered white-bearded Joaquin Miller, doggerel poet from California and a genuine rough, who had stalked through London a few decades before with a ten-gallon hat, putting the pre-Raphaelites in a tizzy. But as far as Pound was concerned, the cowboy impression was more apparent than real. Though born in Idaho, he had left it as a small boy and had been reared in a sedate Philadelphia suburb. And he was quite a different being from Joaquin Miller.

To be sure, there had been a few pioneers among the Poundian ancestors. His grandfather Thaddeus Coleman Pound, lumberman and railway builder, served as congressman from Wisconsin and used to wrestle with his lumberjacks—"not only for sport, but to maintain his prestige," Ezra Pound wrote. Thaddeus Coleman Pound had entered Congress a rich man and left it a poor one (reversing the Lyndon B. Johnson pattern). Arguing for a bill establishing Indian schools, he told the House, "Give them spades instead of powder, plows in place of guns, opportunity rather than hymns and prayers." The same practicality and sense of public responsibility appear in his grandson.

Thaddeus Coleman Pound started as a penniless schoolteacher, founded his own Union Lumbering Company, and built it up to a million-dollar business annually. The Union Lumbering Company's activities stretched over a vast expanse of territory. It cut timber, made it into boards, shingles, and laths, and sold it on wharves along the Mississippi. It even issued its own scrip, good as money in the Company mills and stores. Ezra Pound heard much about the Union Lumbering Company when he was a boy (he was still talking about it at Saint Elizabeth's), and the memory of this great paternalistic state-within-a-state must have influenced his own attitudes: the admiration for Mussolini, the pioneering spirit—in Ezra's case in the cultural field—and the concern for money reform. He had a sample of Union Lumbering Company scrip made into a post card, and used it for correspondence during the nineteen-thirties.

Thaddeus Coleman Pound's wife was of the New York state Loomis family, who, Ezra Pound reports in *Indiscretions*, were "horse-thieves, charming people, in fact, the 'nicest' people in the country, but horse-thieves, very good horse-thieves, never, I think, brought to book." And historical research has shown that this was no poetic exaggeration! Ezra Pound's mother, born Isabel Weston, was of more "solid and respectable" stock: a New England Brahmin family that in colonial times had founded Weston, Massachusetts. Through his mother, Pound was even distantly related to Henry Wadsworth Longfellow—a fact he never boasted of (D. H. Lawrence declared Pound was trying to live it down).

Ezra Pound was born October 30, 1885, in the heart of the Wild West: Hailey, Idaho, whose single street boasted a plank sidewalk, forty-seven bars, one hotel, and a single newspaper. His father, Homer Pound, had moved there to open a Government Land Office for registering mining claims. At four Ezra was taken to Philadelphia, where Homer Pound became assistant assayer of the United States Mint. As a boy Ezra watched gold and silver being assayed, smelted, and made into coins. The origin of his later pre-occupation with money economics is not hard to find here. And a half-century later, remembering his childhood, he even traced his interest in literary quality to that experi-ence: "I like the idea of [testing] the fineness of the metal, and it moves by analogy to the habit of testing *verbal* mani-festations." In *Indiscretions,* Pound gives a delightfully boisterous description of his own ancestry and boyhood. Members of his family appear thinly veiled by pseud-onyms; he himself is "the Infant Gargantua."

Pound grew up in a white shingle house in staid Wyn-cote, Pennsylvania, near Philadelphia. The family was solid middle-class. They were rather loosely Quaker, Dorothy Pound told me. The Quakerism had come to Homer Pound from the side of his paternal grandfather Elijah. Desmond Chute, who knew the younger and older Pounds in Rapallo, wrote: "If Ezra owed to his father that disarm-ing simplicity so inextricably interwoven with his own sophistication, from his mother he derived more striking characteristics: a fine carriage, a springy walk, a sibyline poise of the head, an occasional wilfulness in not admitting or even seeing the other side."

At twelve, Ezra was taken on a European tour by a great-aunt, an enthusiastic creature who "believed that travel

broadened the mind" and had only one adjective to describe all the sights seen: "beautiful."

> but at least she saw damn all Europe
> and rode on that mule in Tangiers
> and in general had a run for her money

(A photograph of the redoubtable great-aunt astride the
mule remained in Ezra Pound's possession; I saw it sixty-
seven years later in his room at Brunnenburg.)

The high point of the trip for the boy seems to have
been Venice. He often returned, and said in 1964, "I first
saw Venice in 1898 and have always wanted to come back.
It has never disappointed me." I suspect that what the
young Ezra saw on this trip cut deep into his consciousness
and gave him a bent toward the splendors of old Europe. It
is hard for a sensitive person to visit Venice and remain
unimpressed.

Contrary to the cliché that geniuses rebel against their
parents, Pound was always close to his. He affectionately
called his father "the naivest man that ever had sound
sense." He regarded his mother (Dorothy Pound told me)
as the most discerning person in her rather limited Philadelphia environment. Her home was pleasantly furnished; she
was sensitive to the arts, though her taste was that of her
generation in America. About 1930 Ezra Pound's father
and mother went to live near him in Italy; both died there
in the nineteen-forties. Sir Max Beerbohm, who lived in
Rapallo too, described Ezra Pound's relations with his parents: "He idolized them, and they idolized him." Not at all
according to Freud!

Pound's headstrong, self-confident character seems to
have been formed at an early age. By fifteen he had conceived the idea of "making a general survey"—inventory-
ing and weighing for himself the best in all world culture;

at that age he entered the University of Pennsylvania "with the intention of studying comparative values in literature (poetry)," he subsequently wrote. He ended with an M.A. there in 1906, after several years at Hamilton College in upstate New York, Loomis horse-thief country. He was a precocious student of romance language, and trained his poet's ear on that most musical of verse, Provençal. By twenty, Pound had begun planning the work that became his epic poem *The Cantos*. The idea, he said, originated in a talk with J. D. Ibbotson, professor at Hamilton.

What was Pound like in those days? He was looking forward confidently, sure of himself. "I knew at fifteen pretty much what I wanted to do," he said later. "I resolved that at thirty I would know more about poetry than any man living, that I would know the dynamic content from the shell, that I would know what was accounted poetry everywhere, what part of poetry was 'indestructable,' what part could *not be lost* by translation, and—scarcely less important—what effects were obtainable in *one* language only. . . ." No modest aims! This ambition made Pound enormously eager to learn, a trait which stayed with him all his life. He was basically shy, but hearty and good-humored, headstrong and impatient of mediocrity. In order to show that he was different—which he was—he dressed according to his own wishes. At Hamilton he wore a big hat with a plume on it through the school year, William Carlos Williams recalled.

On a radio broadcast in honor of Pound's seventieth birthday in 1955, Archibald MacLeish read a letter from a Hamilton professor which gives a vivid glimpse of Pound during his college days: "I believe Dr. X and I saw him more frequently at our houses than did other members of the faculty. He came to my house rather often. Sometimes at a rather unusual hour. Thus one evening in his senior

year, at 11:40, my doorbell rang, and there was Ezra.
'Coming from Utica, I saw a light in your study, the only
welcoming light on Colored Street. May I come in?' We
sat by the fire, and I had a lot of locust wood which burned
with a blue flame, and we smoked and talked until nearly
three o'clock. A good deal about Ossian. He had picked up
an old German translation from the English of MacPherson
and was enthusiastic, and the talk was of Anglo-Saxon
poetry." Another Ezraic vignette from the same letter:
"Calling on a colleague of mine, he asked if he might go to
the bathroom; after a half-hour or more he came down,
having enjoyed a good hot bath in the middle of his call."

While at the University of Pennsylvania, Pound formed
friendships with two students later poets of note: William
Carlos Williams and Hilda Doolittle (H.D.). Williams
wrote his mother about this time: "Pound is a fine fellow;
he is the essence of optimism and has a cast-iron faith that is
something to admire. . . . But not one person in a thousand likes him, and a good many people detest him and
why? Because he is so darned full of conceits and affection. . . . His friends must be all patience in order to find
him out and even then you must not let him know it, for he
will immediately put on some artificial mood, and be really
unbearable. It is too bad, for he loves to be liked, yet there
is some quality which makes him too proud to try to please
people." Pound was then writing a daily sonnet, which he
destroyed at the end of the year, Williams relates in his
autobiography. And Williams records the young Pound's
effect on him: "Before meeting Pound is like B.C. and A.D."
His warm friendship with Pound—personal and literary—
was to last nearly sixty years.

Pound was even for a while engaged to Hilda Doolittle
—which lasted only until Papa Doolittle, professor of
astronomy at the University of Pennsylvania, pronounced

his verdict to Pound: "Why, you're nothing but a no-mad!" After Pound moved to London, Hilda Doolittle gravitated there too, and her lapidary poems in the Greek vein inspired Pound to launch the Imagist movement.

Pound crossed the Atlantic in 1906 to get material for a thesis on Lope de Vega, and tramped about Spain, Prov-ence, and Italy. The walks in Provence, troubadour coun-try, are remembered in "Provincia Deserta":

> I have lain in Rocafixada,
>   level with sunset,
> Have seen the copper come down
>   tingeing the mountains,
> I have seen the fields, pale, clear as an emerald.
> Sharp peaks, high spurs, distant castles.

There are no lovelier romantic lines. "After World War One, Provence was ruined," Pound said to me at Saint Eliz-abeth's.

On his return to America in 1907, he took a teaching job at Wabash College in "the Athens of the West," Craw-fordsville, Indiana—"a town with literary traditions," Pound reported ironically, "Lew Wallace, author of *Ben-Hur*, having died there." The job was short-lived, as may be imagined. After four months he was fired, charged with various misdemeanors—"all accusations having been ulti-mately refuted, save that of being the Latin Quarter type," said Pound.

The immediate cause of his dismissal was that he had fed and lodged a penniless girl from a stranded burlesque show, whom he had found in a blizzard. Pound departed for classes early the next morning and the landlady went to his room to make the bed; she discovered the sleeping girl; she telephoned the president of the college. Pound wrote his friend Williams: "If you ever get degraded, branded with infamy, etc., for feeding a person who needs food, you will probably rise up and bless the present and sacred name of Madame Grundy for all her holy hypocrisy. I am not getting bitter. . . ." But he perhaps was. He departed America and, save for two visits, did not return until Saint Elizabeth's.

Pound landed in Gibraltar with eighty dollars in his pocket, and made his way to Venice—"an excellent place to come to from Crawfordsville, Indiana," he wrote. There his first book of poems was printed at his own expense in an edition of one hundred copies—*A Lume Spento* (*With Quenched Tapers*, a citation from Dante describing the Christian burial ceremony for heathens). A swishy *fin de siècle* Swinburnian tone was prominent here, though Pound had also learned from Browning, Dante, and the troubadours. His old friends Williams and Hilda Doolittle received the book coolly, but William Butler Yeats, the leading poet of London, subsequently called it "charming." In Venice Pound became "European concert tour manager" for Katherine Ruth Heyman, a pianist fifteen years his senior whom he had known in the States, a noted interpreter of Scriabin. By that time, Pound's own artistic taste was not much further advanced than Scriabin's strenuous romanticism. Miss Heyman's concert tour ended in England, and there Pound remained. "I entered London more or less under her wing," he wrote later. He had three pounds when he arrived in London, and knew nobody there.

2

A Yank Among the Georgians

London was Pound's Mecca, and he plunged into the literary life of the metropolis with gusto. "There is no town like London to make one feel the vanity of all art except the highest," he wrote Williams. Before long, he came to know Yeats—and it was through Olivia Shakespear, Dorothy Pound told me. At a tea party in the home of a Mrs. Fowler, an American lady married to an Englishman, Pound had met Olivia Shakespear and her daughter Dorothy, whom he eventually married. Olivia Shakespear had always liked poets and cultivated their acquaintance, and "she rather took to E. P.," Dorothy Pound recalled. She brought him to Yeats' Monday evening "at homes" in Woburn Buildings, literary gatherings of a great pleasantness and charm, for Yeats was a good host. Those evenings are affectionately recorded in *The Pisan Cantos:*

> and the idea that CONversation. . . .
> should not utterly wither
> even I can remember
> at 18 Woburn Buildings
> Said Mr Tancred
> of the Jerusalem and Sicily Tancreds, to Yeats,

"If you would read us one of your own choice
and
       perfect
           lyrics."
and more's the pity that Dickens died twice
with the disappearance of Tancred

Pound found a job teaching romance language literature at the Regent Street Polytechnic and Dorothy Pound attended his lectures, which formed the basis of his coruscant first critical book, *The Spirit of Romance* (1910).

Pound's *A Quinzaine for This Yule* appeared in fall 1908 in an edition of a hundred copies. And then in spring 1909 Elkin Mathews, printer of Yeats' works, published *Personae of Ezra Pound*, a verse collection. Later Pound liked to describe the scene in Mathews' workshop:

> MATHEWS: Ah, eh, ah, would you be prepared to assist in the publication?
> E. P.: I've a shilling in my clothes, if that's any use to you.
> MATHEWS: "Oh, well, I want to publish 'em anyhow.

Pound told me that he and Mathews measured out the poems with calipers so there would be no awkward breaks at the ends of lines and pages. (*Personae* shows the traces of this treatment even in the present edition; apparently Pound did the same with the poems added later. The present-day book called *Personae* has only thirteen poems from the original edition. It was reissued in 1926 and 1949 with enormous changes.)

Personae soon became something of a sensation in London literary circles; Pound's suave irony and impeccable ear for verbal music gave him a modest fame. Yeats quickly recognized the superiority of Pound's ear. In a letter to Lady Gregory (December 10, 1909) he mentions "this queer creature Ezra Pound, who has become really a great authority on the troubadours [and] as I think got closer to the right sort of music for poetry than Mrs. Emery—it is more definitely music with strong marked time and yet it is effective speech." Another collection of Pound's verse, *Exultations*, was published by Elkin Mathews in autumn 1909, and *Canzoni of Ezra Pound* two years later. Mathews' publications seem to have been strictly honorary, for Pound declared in 1913 "I have not yet received a brass farthing for these books."

Personae was very good for its time. Many London reviewers praised it. *The Daily Chronicle* said: "All his poems are . . . from beginning to end, and in every way, his own, and in a world of his own. For brusque intensity of effect, we can hardly compare them to any other work. It is the old miracle that cannot be defined, nothing more than a subtle entanglement of words, so that they rise out of their graves and sing." But Pound was hunting "the white stag, Fame," and did not rely on his poetry alone to win himself a name.

London literary life was a rough-and-tumble, with many literary personages and groups scrambling for predominance, all wanting to be noticed. "Others were modern too, but without changing anything," as Mrs. Pound put it. A poet of talent had to fight his way up, and self-publicizing was one way. So, like many of his artist contemporaries, Pound sought to attract attention by dressing and behaving in the good old *épater les bourgeois* spirit. (Of course poverty had something to do with his weird dress too.) Other poets did the same. Dorothy Pound recalled to me: "It was *not* Ezra who wore the green trousers, as the story goes. No, no, not Ezra! Richard Aldington had the green trousers."

Sorrel-bearded, outlandishly garbed, with one earring

flopping across a cheek, Pound became the center of cultivated gatherings. He was attempting to conquer London
literary society as Oscar Wilde had several decades before,
and he apparently heeded that writer's dictum "the only
thing worse than being talked about is not being talked
about." The earring *got* talked about.

But the buffoonery was only a show. Pound was extremely serious in his purpose: to renovate English verse.
"In a country in love with amateurs . . . it is well that one
man should have a vision of perfection and that he should
be sick to the death and disconsolate because he cannot
attain it," he wrote, and "It is impossible to talk about perfection without getting yourself much disliked." Yet his vision
of perfection concerned more the writing of others than his
own writing. Pound began early to play the role of literary
entrepreneur with a selflessness that distinguished him for
decades afterward. T. S. Eliot, who himself had much to be
grateful for, wrote of Pound:

> He liked to be the impresario for younger men, as well
> as the animator of artistic activity in any milieu in
> which he found himself. In this role he would go to any
> lengths of generosity and kindness, from inviting con-
> stantly to dinner a struggling author whom he sus-
> pected of being under-fed, or giving away clothing
> (though his shoes and underwear were almost the only
> garments which resembled those of other men suffi-
> ciently to be worn by them), to trying to find jobs, col-
> lect subsidies, get work published and then get it criti-
> cised and praised.

English poetry was then dominated by the "Georgians,"
vapid versifiers who sang the joys of country life from
their desks in the city. Pound said later, with some colorful
exaggeration: "The common verse of Britain from 1890
was a horrible agglomerate compost, not minted, most of it

not even baked, all legato, a doughy mess of third-hand Keats, Wordsworth, heaven knows what, fourth-hand Elizabethan sonority blunted, half-melted, lumpy." With his native American directness, he set about the task of bringing excellence back into English verse.

"I'm sick to loathing of artists who don't care for the master work," he declared, and in a burst of bravado doubtless partly humorous, wrote the Georgian poet Lascelles Abercrombie: "Stupidity carried beyond a certain point becomes a public menace," challenging him to a duel. Abercrombie replied suggesting that they bombard each other with unsold copies of their own books at twenty paces (so the story goes)—and there the matter ended.

At Saint Elizabeth's, years later, Pound told me that he settled in London because he wanted to meet Swinburne, Ford Madox Hueffer (later Ford Madox Ford), and William Butler Yeats. With Hueffer and Yeats he did indeed form enduring literary friendships. Pound found Hueffer editing *The English Review* and genially advocating, to anyone who would listen, clarity and directness in prose, and verse "as well written as good prose." Most of Hueffer's ideas on writing were dispensed through conversation, which he loved. After Pound "fell into Ford's hands," as Dorothy Pound said to me, that fluent and inventive novelist taught him to use a natural language in verse—"nothing, *nothing*, that you couldn't in some circumstances, in the stress of some emotion, *actually* say," Pound wrote Harriet Monroe.

Fat Hueffer was a strange character: amiable and society-loving and a colossal prevaricator, a genius at observation who commanded the language like very few of his contemporaries, but always a bit diffuse, a bit *too* much the dilettante. Hemingway has unforgettably portrayed him "breathing heavily through a heavy, stained mustache and holding himself upright as an ambulatory, well clothed, up-ended hogshead." Through his influence on Pound and others, he is in fact the key figure in modern English letters, the pivot on which the work of renovation moved.

Pound and Hueffer became fast and durable friends. "The kindest-hearted man who ever cut a throat," Hueffer called Pound. In *The Pisan Cantos* Pound remembers his talk, better than Yeats' because bound to objective things

> and for all that old Ford's conversation was better,
> consisting in *res* non *verba*,
>> despite William's anecdotes, in that Fordie
>> never dented an idea for a phrase's sake
> and had more humanitas

And Yeats too became a lifelong friend. During his first London years, Pound was, very generally speaking, Yeats' disciple, and the lyrics of the twenty-years-older Irish poet obviously affected his own early verse. However, in the end Pound led Yeats to change his own way of writing, toward a less romantic style "cold and passionate as the dawn." Pound himself declared that his influence on Yeats consisted simply of transmitting Hueffer's ideas to him. Since Hueffer and Yeats could not endure each other, Pound served as intermediary; he would (he said at Saint Elizabeth's) argue with Hueffer in the morning and Yeats in the evening.

A few weeks after *Personae*'s first appearance, Pound met T. E. Hulme, a big, rowdy fellow fresh out of Cambridge, "capable of kicking a theory as well as a man downstairs when the occasion demanded," Jacob Epstein said of him. And this meeting gave another decisive turn to Pound's verse. Hulme was evolving a new philosophy of literature amid the bucolic effusions of the Georgian poets. Like Hueffer, he was disseminating his ideas through con-

versation. On March 25, 1909, Hulme and six others began
meeting weekly to discuss literature at a cheap restaurant in
Soho, London's Latin Quarter. The gatherings were inspired by a disgust with the romantic slushiness then
prevalent in verse. On April 22, Pound—"very full of his
troubadours," F. S. Flint reported—joined the group.

Hulme's posthumously published *Speculations*, gathered
from his notes by Herbert Read and published in 1924,
give an idea of his conversation at that time. They are a
trumpet call for a new age in English poetry—though
Hulme was hardly a trumpet-puffing cherubim. With
astonishing accuracy Hulme predicted that his century
would see a period of dry, hard, classical verse, and defined
classical: "Even in the most imaginative flights there is always a holding back, a reservation. The classical poet never
forgets this finiteness, this limit of man. He remembers
always that he is mixed up with earth." Distinguishing between the classic and the romantic work, Hulme wrote:
"In the classic it is always the light of ordinary day, never
the light that never was on land or sea." "Everything tends
to be angular," Hulme also said, a sentence that Kitasono
Katue often cited in Japan four decades later. Pound's own
verse was in fact moving toward hardness and angularity, a
development which his attendance at weekly gatherings
with Hulme's coterie surely helped bring about.

For his part, Pound made Hulme share his own enthusiasm for poetic precision. He told Hulme about the verse of
Guido Cavalcanti, Dante's contemporary and friend, who
"thought in accurate terms" and whose "phrases correspond to definite sensations undergone," and compared
Guido's precise metaphors to Petrarch's merely decorative
ones. Pound reported that "Hulme took some time over it
in silence, and then finally said: 'That is very interesting';
and after a pause: 'That is more interesting than anything I

ever read in a book.' " (Pound prized Hulme's pause before deciding, for he always hated snap judgments and flippancy. "Slowness is beauty"—the phrase recurs in *The Pisan Cantos.*)

Pound went back to the States during 1910. After a few months with his parents in Wyncote, he moved to New York City. There he prowled the city with eagerness, and praised it in verse

> My City, my beloved, my white! Ah, slender,
> Delicately upon the reed, attend me!
> Listen! Listen to me, and I will breathe into thee a soul.

He explored everywhere, saw everyone he could. With the painter John Butler Yeats, the poet's father, he went to Coney Island, and later recalled "Yeats père on an elephant (at Coney Island), smiling like Elijah in the beatific vision." But he had seen London. New York was too provincial for him. If this was an attempt to strike roots, it failed. By spring 1911 Pound was back in London.

At that time American poetry was almost nonexistent. But meanwhile . . .

In 1911 Harriet Monroe returned to America from a trip around the world. She had purchased Pound's *Personae* and *Exultations* at Elkin Mathews' shop in London, and read them with enthusiasm on the Trans-Siberian Railway. In China she was much impressed with the recognition given poets, and she returned to her homeland inspired to do something for American poetry. Fifty backers were found, who pledged one hundred dollars each, and in 1912 Miss Monroe founded *Poetry: A Magazine of Verse* in Chicago. She wrote Pound asking him to be the magazine's unsalaried "foreign editor." He accepted:

> Dear Madam: I *am* interested, and your scheme as far as I understand it seems not only sound, but the only pos-

sible method. There is no other magazine in America which is not an insult to the serious artist and to the dignity of his art.

But? Can you teach the American poet that poetry *is* an *art*, an art with a technique, with media, an art that must be in constant flux, a constant change of manner, if it is to live? Can you teach him that it is not a pentametric echo of the sociological dogma printed in last year's magazines? Maybe. Anyhow you have work before you.

I may be myopic, but during my last tortured visit to America I found no writer and but one reviewer who had any worthy conception of poetry, The Art. . . .

And he concluded: "I hope . . . to carry into American poetry the same kind of life and intensity Whistler infused into modern painting." Pound threw himself into editing work with customary energy, bombarding Miss Monroe with manuscripts of Yeats, Richard Aldington, H.D., and the Bengali poet Rabindranath Tagore.

Tagore was Pound's first "discovery"—at least as far as America was concerned. He introduced Tagore's verse to the United States in *Poetry*, and called attention to him in critical articles on both sides of the Atlantic. In this case recognition was immediate: Tagore won the Nobel Prize for Literature in 1913. For Pound it was "a damn good smack for the British Academic Committee, who had turned down Tagore on account of his biscuit complexion." But when Tagore became a craze, the center of a pseudo-mystical cultism, Pound lost interest in him. (Pound was like that throughout his life; he would not rest on his laurels, but kept moving on.) He wrote Louis Untermeyer in 1932 that he had backed Tagore "as literary artist *not* as messiah."

Hilda Doolittle had appeared in London in 1911, and

now Pound sent a batch of her poems on to Miss Monroe with praise which characterized his own taste as well as H.D.'s verse: "This is the sort of American stuff that I can show here and in Paris without its being ridiculed. Objective—no slither; direct—no excessive use of adjectives, no metaphors that won't permit examination. It's straight talk, straight as the Greek! And it was only by persistence that I got to see it at all." After much hesitation, Miss Monroe agreed to print H.D.

Now an American poet, Robert Frost—canny, humane, and full of the farmer's mother wit—moved to England, discouraged by the fact that he was nearing forty and still could not get his verse published in the United States. Frost's first volume, *A Boy's Will*, appeared in London in 1913. Pound was one of the book's first readers, and he wrote Harriet Monroe: "Have just discovered another Amur'kn. VURRY Amur'k'n, with, I think, the seeds of grace." Then Pound warmly reviewed the book for *The New Freewoman* in London. "[Frost] is without sham and affectation," he wrote, and began booming Frost wherever and whenever he could—a debt Frost repaid forty-five years later by leading the efforts to get Pound out of Saint Elizabeth's. "It is a sinister thing that so American, I might even say so parochial, a talent as that of Robert Frost should have to be exported before it can find due encouragement and recognition," Pound said. Pound was the first writer of any standing to recognize Frost. As much as anyone, he helped establish Frost's name.

However, Pound was having no easy going in London. Though some admired and liked him, he irritated many. Wyndham Lewis has recorded that he mixed with British society like oil and water, for he was "violently American," a type toward which the English are particularly antipathetic. Pound wrote Harriet Monroe about this time:

"I've got a right to be severe. For one man I strike there are ten to strike back at me. I stand exposed. It hits me in my dinner invitations, in my weekends, in reviews of my own work. Nevertheless it's a good fight." Oscar Wilde had said that one cannot be too careful in the choice of one's enemies. Pound was winning himself a select group of them.

All Pound's own verse was now appearing in *Poetry*. His reading of Catullus, Propertius, and Horace had borne fruit in a style quite his own: lighter, more elliptic. Yeats' influence had been shaken off. The poems subsequently collected in *Lustra* (1915) have a buoyant texture and glancing suggestivity that is something new in English verse:

> And the days are not full enough
> And the nights are not full enough
> And life slips by like a field mouse
>   Not shaking the grass.

Pound acquired a following among *Poetry*'s readers. One concrete result of this was an unexpected commission, which delighted him: to prepare for publication the manuscript translations of Ernest Fenollosa.

That brilliant unacademic scholar had died in 1908 after a life that Pound called "the romance par excellence of modern scholarship." A Massachusetts man summoned to Japan in 1878 as a professor of rhetoric, he came to love the old Japanese art at a time when it was being abandoned or even wantonly destroyed in the first frenzy of Westernization. By his example and persuasion, Fenollosa induced the Japanese to again cherish their own ancient art; in effect, he saved Japanese art for the Japanese. He became Imperial Commissioner of Arts, and his personal art collection is now the Fenollosa-Weld Collection at the Boston Museum of Fine Arts.

Fenollosa's widow had seen Pound's verse in *Poetry*, and

in 1913 she entrusted him with her husband's draft translations of Chinese verse and Japanese Noh drama. From these
Pound produced some of the most clean-cut beauty in English literature. The finely wrought renditions of classic Japanese drama so impressed Yeats that henceforth he wrote
his plays in Noh style. When Yeats saw Pound's redaction
of the Noh translations, he exclaimed (Dorothy Pound
told me): "This is what I have been looking for all my
life!" At Saint Elizabeth's I asked Pound what he had done
to the Fenollosa manuscripts. "Just took out some of the
Victorian language," he replied—a great excess of modesty,
as the reader may see by comparing Pound's versions and
the Fenollosa drafts quoted later in this book. Without sacrificing their sense, Pound carved Fenollosa's notes into
durable verse.

Poetry magazine had established a $250 prize for the best
poem published in the magazine each year, and the first
went to Yeats for his poem "The Grey Rock." Yeats
would accept only $50 of the award, and asked that the
rest be given to some more needy young poet of talent.
Then he reconsidered, and wrote Miss Monroe:

> Why not give the £40 to Ezra Pound? I suggest him to
> you because, although I do not really like with my
> whole soul the metrical experiments he has made for
> you, I think those experiments show a vigorous creative
> mind. He is certainly a creative personality of some
> sort, though it is too soon yet to say of what sort. His
> experiments are perhaps errors, I am not certain; but I
> would always sooner give the laurel to vigorous errors
> than to any orthodoxy not inspired.

And Pound welcomed the money. His subsistence during
these years was terribly uncertain, his survival—as he said
many decades later—"a miracle of God."

Yeats had begun to be a kind of sponsor for Pound. The

effects were crucial—but on Yeats rather than on Pound. During the winters of 1913–1914, 1914–1915, and 1915–1916, Pound served Yeats as secretary in a Sussex cottage, discussing with him, reading to him, and writing to dictation. Yeats wrote Lady Gregory an interesting testimonial about his secretary:

> He is full of the middle ages and helps me to get back to the definite and concrete away from modern abstractions. To talk over a poem with him is like getting you to put a sentence into [Irish] dialect. All becomes clear and natural. Yet in his own work he is very uncertain, often very bad though very interesting sometimes. He spoils himself by too many experiments and has more sound principles than taste.

In these years Yeats' style changed so radically that critics write of "early Yeats" and "late Yeats" almost as if two different poets were being described—and much of the credit must go to Pound. Conversely, Pound's prose and his versions of the Noh plays, composed at this time, have the ring of Yeats' diction.

With other American and British poets then in London —Richard Aldington, Hilda Doolittle, F. S. Flint—Pound now founded a literary group that called itself "Les Imagistes." Aldington writes in his autobiography *Life for Life's Sake* that Pound was so excited about some new poems of H.D. that he summoned them all to his flat in Kensington and declared they were "Imagistes." The "image" Pound defined as "that which presents an intellectual and emotional complex in an instant of time." This definition helped form another gifted poet who soon appeared in London, the greatest of the Imagists though he never belonged to the group: T. S. Eliot.

Poetry magazine published "An Interview with an Imagiste." The interviewer was F. S. Flint, the anonymous interviewee, Pound. Here Pound defined the aims of the group: (1) direct treatment of the subject (which meant that Imagist verse was often strongly visual); (2) use of no superfluous words; (3) composition "in sequence of the musical phrase, not in sequence of a metronome" (so-called free verse). "To break the iamb—that was the first heave," Pound wrote some years later. After this statement of principles, *Poetry* printed a signed article by Pound, "A Few Don'ts by an Imagist." Some bits of timeless advice were offered to poets: "Pay no attention to the criticism of men who have never themselves written a notable work. . . . Go in fear of abstractions. . . . Be influenced by as many great artists as you can, but have the decency either to acknowledge the debt outright, or try to conceal it."

Now Pound anonymously edited an anthology entitled, in somewhat dubious French, *Des Imagistes*, which appeared in March 1914. Pound gave the most space to Aldington and H.D., and included himself and eight others. Pound's predilection for anonymity at this time is worth noting. It is a good refutation of the idea that he was a big self-advertiser, in poetry mainly to boom his own name. In fact, he never was.

Pound was concentrating on sharpening his eye. What he called *phanopoeia*—visual poetry—is predominant throughout *Lustra* (1915). His two-line "In a Station of the Metro" has been quoted and quoted "to the mystical point of dullness"—and is still one of the profoundest of images. In *T.P.'s Weekly* for June 6, 1913, Pound described how this poem came about:

> For well over a year I have been trying to make a poem of a very beautiful thing that befell me in the Paris Underground. I got out of a train at, I think, La Concorde and in the jostle I saw a beautiful face, and then, turning suddenly, another and another, and then a beautiful child's face, and then another beautiful face. All that

day I tried to find words for what this made me feel. That night as I went home along the rue Raynouard I was still trying. I could get nothing but spots of colour. I remember thinking that if I had been a painter I might have started a wholly new school of painting. I tried to write the poem weeks afterwards in Italy, but found it useless. Then only the other night, wondering how I should tell the adventure, it struck me that in Japan, where a work of art is not estimated by its acreage and where sixteen syllables are counted enough for a poem if you arrange and punctuate them properly, one might make a very little poem which would be translated about as follows:—

> The apparition of these faces in the crowd;
> Petals on a wet, black bough

And there, or in some other very old, very quiet civilisation, some one else might understand the significance.

The lesson: poetry is *Dichtung*, condensation.

Reinforcements for Imagism soon arrived on the scene. John Gould Fletcher, a wealthy American living in London, began calling himself "Imagiste." Pound sent his verse on to *Poetry*. Meanwhile plump, cigar-puffing Amy Lowell of Brookline, Massachusetts, appeared in London to jump on the Imagist bandwagon—and nearly tipped it over. "Our only hippo-poetess," Pound called her in a letter; "a kind of demon saleswoman" wrote T. S. Eliot. She began advertising herself as the Imagists' leader, and before long Pound dissociated himself from the group, declaring that "Imagism" had become "Amy-gism." Miss Lowell and Fletcher avenged themselves with acid attacks on Pound, who, as usual, replied with gusto and good humor, showing himself a much better sport than his adversaries. "Imagism" became the rage among English and American poets for several decades—but by then Pound had traveled far beyond it.

3

Blast and After

Pound having outgrown (or outsquabbled) Imagism, the next *ism* exploded with a *BLAST*: it was called Vorticism, and *BLAST* was "A Review of the Great English Vortex," edited by Wyndham Lewis. "This puce monster," as Lewis proudly called it after the cover color of the first number, survived two rancorous issues but was laid low by a real and terrible blast, the First World War. Pound, Lewis, Aldington, and eight others released a Vorticist manifesto damning Victorianism and a number of other things, quarreled among themselves, quarreled with others, and succeeded in antagonizing most of the English intellectual public—which was precisely their aim. By all the sound and fury, they hoped to start a whirl of artistic production, one artist stimulating another to creation—a "vortex"—as had made the great civilizations of the past: Egypt, Greece, and China. Perhaps they stirred up more dust than anything else. (When Lewis died in 1958, the New York *Herald Tribune* obituary called his movement "Verticism." And indeed there *was* something vertiginous in it!)

Lewis was a man of great energy and Germanic intellectual heaviness—a twentieth-century Carlyle—prolific as both writer and painter. Hemingway said he looked like an ugly frog. His friendship with Pound lasted till the end, despite the self-assertiveness of both men. Mrs. Pound told me that, beneath the hardness, Lewis would sometimes be unexpectedly gentle—as once when, much to her embarrassment, he caught her painting. With much kindliness and tact, he pointed out places where the work might be improved. Lewis' painting is sharp and cold, but his portraits of Eliot and Pound show that he does see with the inner as well as the outer eye, for they superbly convey their subjects' temperaments.

Now Pound was often with a handsome oval-faced lady, Dorothy Shakespear, daughter of Yeats' lifelong friend Olivia Shakespear. They were married in April 1914, and Pound took his bride down to the estate of Wilfred Scawen Blunt, the poet mentioned in a celebrated passage of *The Pisan Cantos:*

> To have, with decency, knocked
> That a Blunt should open
>   To have gathered from the air a live tradition
> or from a fine old eye the unconquered flame
> This is not vanity.
>   Here error is all in the not done,
> all in the diffidence that faltered,

Old Blunt, who had seen many years' military service in Egypt, had become intensely involved in public affairs, opposing British imperialism in the Middle East—a curious parallel to the political passions of the poet Pound some decades later. Dorothy Pound recalled to me that the white-bearded Blunt appeared in magnificent Arab robes, drank champagne mixed with water, and took the young couple for a drive in a wagonette. Then the Pounds departed for a wedding trip to Provence, where with rucksacks they walked the hills and byroads of the troubadours and slept outdoors. "Dante was my Baedeker in Provence," wrote Pound—and that tells a lot about his mind.

John Cournos became a close friend. He was a talented art critic and translator of Russian who had tossed over a good job as art critic for a Philadelphia newspaper in order to write what he wanted, and he lived poor as Pound in London. Worthy of note, considering Pound's later bias, is that Cournos was Jewish. Pound introduced him everywhere among his literary friends, was responsible for getting a book of his published, even gave him money (Pound had little enough himself). "One of the kindest men that ever lived," Cournos wrote of Pound. Another of Pound's circle at this time was Jacob Epstein, also Jewish, maker of "Vorticist sculpture." Pound wrote an essay in praise of Epstein's work, and the title of an Epstein piece, "Rock Drill," perhaps gave the name to a section of *The Cantos* written forty years later.

Meanwhile a spare and austere young man just out of Harvard had emigrated to England with a pile of unpublished poems: T. S. Eliot. His verse had appeared only in a Harvard undergraduate magazine. Eliot was employed at Lloyds Bank, and looked the part; Hueffer declared, after seeing him for the first time, "I do not care for bank clerks!" Later, somewhat ruing that rash first judgment, he learned to appreciate Eliot as a poet.

On September 14, 1914, at Conrad Aiken's instigation, Eliot called on Pound at his Kensington apartment and showed him the manuscript of that masterpiece of witty introspection, "The Love Song of J. Alfred Prufrock." As usual, Pound reacted decidedly and immediately—and as usual his judgment has been amply substantiated by time: "The best poem I have yet had or seen from an American," he wrote Harriet Monroe. Pound induced *Poetry* to print Eliot, over strenuous objections by Miss Monroe. She thought "Prufrock" "goes off at the end" (ironically, many critics now consider precisely the last lines to be the poem's finest). Pound wrote her: "No, most emphatically I will not ask Eliot to write down to any audience whatsoever. . . . Nor will I send you Eliot's address in order that he may be insulted." Miss Monroe finally capitulated.

The relations of the editor and "foreign editor" of *Poetry* during these years can best be described as guerrilla warfare. In addition to the wrangle about Eliot, Pound had to hector Miss Monroe into first publishing H.D. and Frost. In December 1913 Pound resigned, saying he would not have his name associated with the magazine unless it improved. She begged him to reconsider. He did. He wrote her damning the magazine's "pink blue baby ribbon" tone. She called parts of his "Contemporanea" series "risqué." He replied in "Ancora":

> Good God! They say you are risqué,
> O canzonetti!
> We who went out into the four A.M. of the world
> Composing our albas,
> We who shook off our dew with the rabbits,
> We who have seen even Artemis a-binding her sandals,
> Have we ever heard the like?

It is instructive to contrast Pound's economic state at this time with that of his contemporaries, lesser American poets who stayed at home, worked at well-paying jobs—and came to nothing as poets. Pound took the harder way. During his early London years an overcoat served him as both clothing and blanket. In 1914, a year of large and brilliant production for him, Pound's total income from writing was £42. "My American royalties amount to about one dollar 85 cents per year," he wrote in 1916. Mrs. Pound told me that his father sent him ten dollars a month for some time (in her book *Ezra Pound's Kensington*, Patricia Hutchins

declares that the family allowance was terminated in 1911),
and Mrs. Pound herself had an annuity of £150 from her
own family. The New York City lawyer John Quinn, this
century's great literary patron, sent Pound money for a few
years after 1915. The Pounds lived in a small dark apartment in Kensington, at eight shillings a week. In the larger
room Pound cooked (with great skill) by artificial light; in
the smaller—better illuminated but of an inconvenient triangular shape—the Pounds received guests. They were
often invited out to meals. Writing itself got Pound little
money. In fact, while he was one of the world's most renowned literary men, his earnings from his writings—until
he was in his sixties—were insignificant. But Pound was
never inclined to brood over his own poverty:

> Come, let us pity those who are better off than we are.
> Come, my friend, and remember
>   that the rich have butlers and no friends,
> And we have friends and no butlers.
> Come, let us pity the married and the unmarried.

In 1915 Pound edited *The Catholic Anthology* ("catholic" used in the sense of "universal") "in order to get fifteen pages of Eliot into print," he declared later. By now
Harriet Weaver and Dora Marsden's suffragette magazine
The New Freewoman had evolved into *The Egoist*, with
Richard Aldington as assistant editor, and most of Pound's
prose was appearing in the magazine—which could not
afford to pay contributors. He and Eliot became "literary
advisers" to *The Egoist*.

Pound always liked people as cantankerous as himself,
even when he did not agree with their ideas, so he and
Aldington had been friends since the days of Imagism,
which Aldington had helped launch at age nineteen.
Aldington was a gifted, imaginative poet of much taste—

"terribly proud of his Greek and Latin," Mrs. Pound recalled of him. He remained in correspondence with Pound
until the last days of his life in 1962. Through Aldington,
Pound, and Eliot, *The Egoist* became very influential in the
English world of letters. It was not long after Pound joined
the magazine in autumn 1913 that he brought an unknown
Irish writer and *The Egoist* into literary history.

James Joyce was then a starveling in Trieste, struggling
to record the Dublin he had abandoned. Pound first heard
of Joyce from Yeats, who showed him Joyce's poem "I
Hear an Army." Both Pound and Yeats were much impressed by it, and Pound wrote Joyce in December 1913,
offering to include "I Hear an Army" in the anthology *Des
Imagistes*—and even to pay for it!—and asking if he had
any other work on hand. This encouraged Joyce to make
the final corrections on the first chapter of *A Portrait of
the Artist as a Young Man* and send it to Pound together
with a copy of *Dubliners*. On January 19, 1914, Pound
wrote Joyce expressing warm approval. He reviewed
Dubliners in *The Egoist*, declaring that it marked a return
of style into English prose—one of the few favorable reviews that *Dubliners* got—and he arranged for *The Egoist*
to publish *A Portrait of the Artist*, first serially and then in
book form.

Pound began making Joyce's reputation and material
welfare his business. In 1915, aided by Yeats, he succeeded
in obtaining a subsidy of £75 for Joyce from the Royal
Literary Fund; also Pound sent him an anonymous gift of
£25 that year and arranged for the Society of Authors to
give him £2 a week. Pound even took to sending Joyce old
clothes, which the Irishman perhaps never wore. Joyce
dressed nattily, and when he had money would spend it on
only the most elegant attire.

Pound had brought Joyce to the attention of *The*

Egoist's publisher Harriet Weaver—indeed "thrust him down her throat," Wyndham Lewis wrote—and subsequently she set aside a sum of money that enabled Joyce to live comfortably in a Paris apartment and finish *Ulysses*. "The magician in this Arabian Nights Tale was undoubtedly Ezra," said Lewis. "Without Pound, the author of the *Portrait of the Artist* would perhaps never have written *Ulysses* or *Finnegan's Wake*." In 1932 Joyce declared of Pound: "Nothing could be more true than to say that we all owe a great deal to him. But I most of all surely. It is nearly twenty years since he first began his vigorous campaign on my behalf and it is probable that but for him I should still be the unknown drudge that he discovered—if it was a discovery." However, by then the two writers had grown far apart.

Pound had always a keen interest in all the arts—he even tried his hand at music composition and sculpting—and in 1913 he took up the cause of Henri Gaudier-Brzeska, a vigorous young French artist who had settled in London. His book *Gaudier-Brzeska* (1916) praises that sculptor's strong forms. Gaudier carved a hieratic head of Pound which remained in the poet's possession together with many drawings and a curled cat of marvelous stony softness. His sketch of Pound is a frontispiece to the present edition of *Personae*.

Pound's next discovery was most fruitful in what it called forth from himself. In Harold Munro's magazine *Poetry and Drama*, he found poems by one Iris Barry. He wrote her asking if he could place some of her work in *Poetry*. She was, it turned out, a seventeen-year-old clerk in the Birmingham Post Office, and she sent him a batch of verse with a request for criticism. There followed a correspondence in which Pound the teacher is seen at his most brilliant. He is unsparingly generous with criticism and with suggestions for reading. Tip follows tip, a whole course in poetry is set forth. The letters to Iris Barry are the genesis of two later Poundian works, surveys of world literature: the essay "How to Read" and the book *The ABC of Reading.*

Miss Barry soon moved to London, where Pound introduced her about, with his usual unflagging kindness toward promising writers. The promise as a poet was not fulfilled, but she wrote a very lively memoir of Pound and his circle in London, published many years later in *The Bookman* (1931). With marvelous exactitude she describes Wyndham Lewis' painting of the master: "It [seized] the essential Ezra. A little larger than life-size, sculptural face (the cat-look is, after all, that of an Egyptian cat), hair in long tongues of fire, the grey coat having wonderfully the perpetual air of majestic flowing and billowing, the inevitable ebony stick, the quizzical expression, the force and dangerousness and simplicity of the man were all in that."

In a letter to John Quinn, January 24, 1917, we find Pound announcing "work on a new long poem (really L O N G, endless, leviathanic)." This was *The Cantos,* a bold and unique venture at writing a modern epic, which Pound had been pondering since 1904. It became his life's work. He accurately predicted that its completion would take half a century. *The Cantos* include all history, with episodes from various periods that seem to Pound most significant in civilization, knit together by the idea of the "repeat in history." The poem contains a bitter attack on the corruption of present civilization, while it attempts to prevent the death of that civilization by gathering together fragments of past and present which the poet considers worthwhile. It very roughly follows Dante's *Divine Comedy,* with an inferno, a purgatory, and a paradise section. The first three Cantos appeared in *Poetry* during 1917, and were later greatly revised by Pound.

Then, in Yeats' thunderous expression, "established

things were shaken by the Great War." Good friends of Pound went off to the trenches: Aldington, Hueffer, Lewis, Gaudier-Brzeska, Hulme. The latter two did not return.

> And Henri Gaudier went to it,
>   and they killed him,
> And killed a good deal of sculpture,
> And ole T.E.H. he went to it,
> With a lot of books from the library,
> London Library, and a shell buried 'em in a dug-out,
> And the Library expressed its annoyance.
>   [Canto 16]

Pound was shocked to see a nation sacrificing its wealth and its young men for . . . nothing. Parts of his poem "Hugh Selwyn Mauberley," published 1920, are a poetic equivalent of Remarque's *All Quiet on the Western Front*. One powerfully compact line sums up the soldiers' experience:

> walked eye-deep in hell

In an autobiographical sketch for *Selected Poems of Ezra Pound*, he writes: "1918 began investigation of causes of war, to oppose same."

Before long, Pound found out what caused war—or thought he did. After *The Egoist* creased in 1919, no English magazine would publish him except A. W. Orage's *The New Age;* he had succeeded in antagonizing one editor after another through that tumultuous decade in London. Orage introduced Pound to "Social Credit," an economic theory recently propounded by Colonel C. H. Douglas, a Scotsman. In Douglas' view, both war and scarcity of money were caused by financiers' manipulations —usury—and his panacea was nationalized credit. Pound became a convert:

with usura
seeth no man Gonzaga his heirs and his concubines
no picture is made to endure nor to live with
but is made to sell and sell quickly
with usura, sin against nature,
is thy bread ever more of stale rags
is thy bread dry as paper,
with no mountain wheat, no strong flour
with usura the line grows thick
with usura is no clear demarcation
and no man can find site for his dwelling.
Stone cutter is kept from his stone
weaver is kept from his loom
WITH USURA

       *   *   *

They have brought whores for Eleusis
Corpses are set to banquet
at behest of usura.
               [Canto 45]

Just why did he take up Social Credit? He was brooding
about the War, groping for an explanation of its senseless-
ness. After the War, revolution was in the air; the same
disgust with the old order that brought about the Russian
Revolution may have impelled Pound's economic interest
too. He was always an intensely social person, very much
alive to his environment and concerned with improving it.
And it should not be forgotten that Pound and most of his
friends were perpetually broke. "If you only make 40
pounds a year, it impresses itself upon you that it's not
enough, and you begin to wonder why," Mrs. Pound observed to me.

Yet Pound had little sympathy for the revolutionaries he
knew. He wrote John Quinn about Maude Gonne, agitator
for Irish independence and Yeats' inamorata: "M. does not
seem quite lunatic. But I notice with Yeats he will be quite

sensible till some question of ghosts or occultism comes up, then he is subject to a curious excitement, twists everything to his theory, usual quality of mind goes. So with M. G." Strangely enough, however, Pound came to the same kind of fanaticism in political and economic matters—and his description of Yeats and Maude Gonne would fit himself!

His own view of his place in things at this time was hardly modest—but if he was presumptuous it was rather about his mission to help other writers than about his own works. He wrote Harriet Monroe: "My problem is to keep alive a certain group of advancing poets, to set the arts in their rightful place as the acknowledged guide and lamp of civilization." And in fact he *was* doing what he claimed, at least helping to do it.

An American magazine, *The Little Review*, offered to make Pound foreign editor, and he accepted, "in order that the work of Joyce, Lewis, Eliot and myself might appear promptly and regularly and in one place, without inane and idiotic delay" (*Little Review*, May 1917). Among the first-fruits harvested by the magazine's new foreign editor was the manuscript of *Ulysses*. *The Little Review* began publishing it serially; whereupon the New York City police stepped in and confiscated an entire issue, on complaint of the Society for the Prevention of Vice. Then, after *Ulysses* finally appeared in book form, customs officials prevented its importation into the United States until the Circuit Court of Appeals decision of 1934. Pound's rage was colossal. He wrote in 1928: "As to Mr. Coolidge's economic policy, I have one further suggestion—namely, that he can completely eliminate the cost of lunatic asylums by dressing the present inmates in customs uniforms and placing them in ports and along the frontiers. This will dispense with the present employees entirely and the public will be just as well served."

In 1918 Pound conceived and edited a *Little Review*

number devoted entirely to Henry James, who had died two years before, ignored by the young and in danger of being forgotten. Pound revered James and had visited him several times in his London home. In Canto 7, composed about this time, he recalls the dead master "with eyes honest and slow," a phrase from Dante:

> The house too thick, the paintings
> a shade too oiled.
> And the great domed head, *con gli occhi onesti e tardi*
> Moves before me, phantom with weighted motion,
> *Grave incessu*, drinking the tone of things,
> And the old voice lifts itself
>   weaving an endless sentence.

About the time of *The Little Review*'s James issue, the upsurge of interest in "the great blagueur" began. James is now a classic, and Pound may be given a good deal of the credit; among others, Hueffer's book on James (1913) helped the resurrection too.

Pound was at the peak of his career as literary impresario when a Brooklyn lady librarian, prim Miss Marianne Moore, sent him poems. They were precise, factual, prosaic, at first glance lacking intensity, but such a cool, civilized sensibility had never been expressed in English verse before. "Make it new" was Pound's poetic principle, and he recognized Miss Moore's freshness. He wrote her, "Your stuff holds my eye. Most verse I merely slide off (God I do ye thank for this automatic selfprotection), BUT my held eye goes forward very slowly. . . ." He got her first book published by the Egoist Press. He urged her to continue with her "definite delineation," and she did. Once again he was years ahead of other critics in his appreciation. (Four decades later, at Saint Elizabeth's, Pound was still helping Miss Moore—this time with encouragement and criticism of her translations from La Fontaine's fables.)

Two poetic sequences, *Homage to Sextus Propertius* (1919) and *Hugh Selwyn Mauberly* (1920) are Pound's valedictories to London, the summation and masterpieces of his pre-*Cantos* work. *Propertius* is a quittance with England and its imperial pomp, *Mauberley* a quittance with himself as pure aesthete. Irony lies deep at the heart of both. *Mauberley*'s is, for the most part, cool:

> All things are a flowing,
> Sage Heracleitus says;
> But a tawdry cheapness
> Shall outlast our days.
>
> * * *
>
> Knowing my coat has never been
> Of precisely the fashion
> To stimulate, in her,
> A durable passion.
>
> * * *
>
> "I was
> And I no more exist;
> Here drifted
> An hedonist."

Propertius' is lusty and full-blooded:

> When, when, and whenever death closes our eyelids,
> Moving naked over Acheron
> Upon the one raft, victor and conquered together,
> Marius and Jugurtha together,
>   one tangle of shadows.
> Caesar plots against India,
> Tigris and Euphrates shall, from now on, flow at his bidding,
> Tibet shall be full of Roman policemen,
> The Parthians shall get used to our statuary
>   and acquire a Roman religion;
> One raft on the veiled flood of Acheron,
>   Marius and Jugurtha together.

The satire of Britain's imperial grandeur is unmistakable. Pound, speaking through the mask of Propertius, will have none of it.

Aldington came back from the trenches and found Pound in a low. He was lying down and complaining of intellectual gout, tapping his Adam's apple and declaring that the brains of the English stopped short there. Now he spleenfully wrote Margaret Anderson: "Chère amie, I am, for the time being, bored to death with being any kind of editor. I desire to go on with my long poem; and like the Duke of Chang, I desire to hear the music of a lost dynasty." By 1920 he was writing his friend William Carlos Williams that there was no intellectual life in England save what centered in his own room.

Pound had, in fact, become fed up with England. Perhaps he shared the disillusion of the soldiers who, as he tells in *Mauberley:*

> came home, home to a lie,
> home to many deceits,
> home to old lies and new infamy;
> usury age-old and age-thick
> and liars in public places.

Or he may have simply grown out of London, so that the English smoothness and polish now went against his Yankee grain. In any case, the romance of the metropolis had worn off. He described British literary life as "a privy," and wrote W. H. D. Rouse some years later: "I know the great English public loves smugness and the great passion of the majority is for a boot, any damn boot, to lick." The "hell" Cantos, 14 and 15, are a portrait of England as it was when he left. His friend Hueffer marveled that Pound, who ten years before had (Hueffer said) bored everyone in Philadelphia with his tireless praises of London literary life, had now become a violent Anglophobe.

4

70 *bis rue Notre-Dame-des-Champs*

In 1921 Pound finally crossed the Channel for good. He had been planning the move all through his last vexed years in London, but the war had held it up.

The Pounds rented an apartment in Paris, at 70 *bis* rue Notre-Dame-des-Champs, the street on which Whistler had lived as a young man. Pound had always admired French letters—Villon, Stendhal, and Flaubert were standards of excellence for him—and at first he moved with delight in the magical Paris ambiance. He talked long with Louis Aragon, translated Cocteau, wrote an appreciation of Brancusi the sculptor, and visited Gertrude Stein—"that amiable fraud," he called her at Saint Elizabeth's. She wrote of Pound: "he was a village explainer, excellent if you were a village, but if you were not, not."

It is no coincidence that while Pound was there, Paris became the center of the best writing in English. Ford Madox Hueffer (who now called himself Ford Madox Ford) soon moved over to Paris too, and founded the *transatlantic review*. And then one day Pound entered Sylvia Beach's book shop Shakespeare & Co. with his wife, and found a lanky young man there, obviously an American, "mousing around the book shelves," Mrs. Pound recalled to me, pulling out one book after another. Miss Beach introduced him: Ernest Hemingway.

At Saint Elizabeth's Pound said that Hemingway told him: "I have traveled four thousand miles to see *you*." The young American showed his manuscript stories to Pound, who declared quite simply that they were something new in American literature. It was Pound, Hemingway said, who taught him "more about how to write and how not to write" than anyone else. Hemingway called Pound "the man who had taught me to distrust adjectives as I would later learn to distrust certain people in certain situations." At Saint Elizabeth's Pound told Rolf Fjelde that he had blue-penciled parts of Hemingway's *In Our Time*.

Pound was then supervising a series of books for the Three Mountains Press, run by an American journalist, William Bird, who printed the books himself on an old hand press on the Isle Saint-Louis. Pound got Hemingway's first novel, *In Our Time*, published by Three Mountains Press, and again did all he could to boom the name of a little-known writer. By way of appreciation, Hemingway wrote in 1925:

> So far we have Pound the major poet devoting, say, one fifth of his time to poetry. With the rest of his time he tries to advance the fortunes, both material and artistic, of his friends. He defends them when they are attacked, he gets them into magazines and out of jail. He loans them money. He sells their pictures. He arranges concerts for them. He writes articles about them. He introduces them to wealthy women. He gets publishers to take their books. He sits up all night with them when they claim to be dying and he witnesses their wills. He advances them hospital expenses and dissuades them

from suicide. And in the end a few of them refrain from knifing him at the first opportunity.

The Hemingways took an apartment just down the street from the Pounds'. Pound had been a fencer since college days, and now he traded fencing lessons for boxing lessons with Hemingway. When they sparred, Hemingway apparently took pains not to kayo the greatest American poet, for (Dorothy Pound said) Ezra complained to him, "You treat me like a piece of Dresden china!"

Pound made the furniture for 70 *bis* rue Notre-Dame-des-Champs himself. The apartment had a cat. Pound was always a great cat lover. (Perhaps there was an affinity; Ramon Guthrie's poem aptly described him as a leopard or a lynx. Others have written of his "cat eyes.") He hammered at oval pieces of marble, split them, and produced Brancusi-type abstractions which lay about the floor. He tried his hand at playing the bassoon. He played a good game of tennis. He was, Hemingway reports, very accessible to visitors. With his scraggly red beard and flowing cape, he was a well-known sight on the Paris streets.

As usual he was very poor in Paris. Fame did not help pay the bills. For a while his poverty was eased when he signed a contract with the American publisher Horace Liveright to translate French literature. This brought in the vast sum (for him) of five hundred dollars. But money was always a problem, and money concerned him more and more—the reform of the money system through Major Douglas' Social Credit theories. He began preaching them to all his literary friends.

In 1920 Pound finally saw James Joyce, whom he had helped for many years. Joyce was still living in Trieste working on his *Ulysses*. They arranged to meet at Sirmione, a village jutting into Lake Garda in north Italy where Catullus had lived. Joyce came with his son, and Pound was much amused when the great writer's arrival was appropriately heralded by a tremendous thunderstorm. In *The Pisan Cantos* we find him

> recalling the arrival of Joyce et fils
> at the haunt of Catullus
> with Jim's veneration of thunder and the
> Gardasee in magnificence

At Pound's instigation, Joyce moved to Paris, where Harriet Weaver set him up with a handsome income so he could write without financial worries and have his ailing eyes treated. Then Pound persuaded the Paris bookstore proprietress Sylvia Beach to enter the publishing business for the sake of bringing out *Ulysses*. And he set about soliciting prepublication subscriptions from everyone he could reach. A look at Bernard Shaw's letters will show what he had to endure for it. "Do I have to do everything you like, Ezra?" Shaw sneered. "As for me, I take care of the pence and let the Pounds take care of themselves." The two writers exchanged a dozen letters about *Ulysses*, each unwilling to let the other have the last word. Shaw remained adamant.

T. S. Eliot was still slaving at Lloyds Bank in London. In 1921 he suffered a breakdown and was sent off for three months' recuperation in Switzerland. There he occupied himself with composing a long poem called "The Waste Land," and on the way back to London deposited it with Pound in Paris, asking for criticism. It was a "sprawling, chaotic" manuscript, Eliot has written—and Pound cut out half, commemorating his own editorial work in this ditty:

> These are the poems of Eliot
> By the Uranian Muse begot;

A Man their Mother was,
A Muse their Sire.

How did the printed Infancies result
From Nuptials thus doubly difficult?

If you must needs enquire
Know diligent Reader
That on each Occasion
Ezra performed the Caesarean Operation. . . .

Eliot published "The Waste Land" as edited, with the famous dedication "To Ezra Pound, *il miglior fabbro*" ("the better smith"—Dante's characterization of the Provençal poet Arnaut Daniel).

Pound declared: "A masterpiece; one of the most important nineteen pages in English." "The Waste Land" soon became very influential in literary circles, and was widely imitated; no piece of writing so movingly sums up contemporary moral chaos. Meanwhile Pound was collecting money for a fund to release Eliot from bank-clerk drudgery and propagandizing for Major Douglas' Social Credit ideas. In his delightful Paris memoirs, *A Moveable Feast*, Hemingway tells how he would tease Pound by pretending to confuse the two enthusiasms and speaking of "Major Eliot."

No one knows the whereabouts of *The Waste Land*'s original manuscript, so drastically cut by Pound. Its mysterious disappearance has never been accounted for. Eliot wrote, indicating that he himself did not know, "I should like to think that the manuscript, with its suppressed passages, had disappeared irrevocably; yet, on the other hand, I should wish the blue pencilling on it to be preserved as irrefutable evidence of Pound's critical genius." One fact is sure: Eliot sent the manuscript to John Quinn, the New York City literary patron, for his manuscript collection. However, when the Quinn collection was dispersed in

1924, the *Waste Land* manuscript was not sold; it was not listed in the catalogue of that sale. It has dropped from sight without a trace.

Pound's college friend William Carlos Williams—now a physician in Rutherford, New Jersey—had become a solid poet, *exceedingly* American, and that was his originality. For decades Pound encouraged Williams and helped him develop as a writer. He recommended Williams to the publisher of his second book, *The Tempers,* and to the editors of such magazines as *The Egoist* and *Poetry.* Williams and Pound swapped genial attacks across the Atlantic, and a kind of poetic cross-pollination apparently ensued: Pound held on to his Americanness, and Williams' poetic principles—conversational diction, the primacy of visual images—became very much like Pound's own. There is more boisterous warmth in Pound's letters to Williams than in any others.

Williams lambasted Pound and Eliot for not staying home to fight with the problems of being a writer in America. Pound's answer is revealing of himself. He wrote Williams in 1920: "There is a blood poison in America; . . . you don't need to fight the disease day and night; you never had to. Eliot has it perhaps worse than I—poor devil. You have the advantage of arriving in the milieu with a fresh flood of Europe in your veins, Spanish, French, English, Danish. You had not the thin milk of New York and New England from the pap; and you can therefore keep the environment outside you, and decently objective." Yet, curiously enough, the longer Pound stayed in Europe, the more he came to assert his own early American origins, the same ones he had called a blood poison. His letters become more and more folksy American; he writes the American history Cantos, 62 to 81. Perhaps this self-assertion was part of a struggle to maintain his individuality as an American in Europe.

Now Pound became Paris editor of the New York magazine *The Dial,* and recognized a fine new poet in E. E. Cummings when *The Dial* first published that astringently tender lyricist. Cummings appeared in Paris, and the two poets strolled together one evening through misty streets. Some thirty-five years later, Cummings wrote Charles Norman, remembering this first meeting with Pound: "During our whole promenade Ezra was more than wonderfully entertaining: he was magically gentle, as only a great man can be toward some shyest child." Cummings became a lifelong friend whom Pound jokingly called "the Kumrad," in commemoration of a brief venture into leftist politics during the early nineteen-thirties.

The latest sensation in Paris then was George Antheil, self-styled "bad boy of music," a good-looking young American composer of towering egotism who carried an automatic pistol in a special pocket sewed under his armpit. The audience rioted at several Paris concerts of his extravagantly modernist music. One was either violently pro-Antheil or violently against. Pound wrote a book of praise, *Antheil, and the Treatise on Harmony* (1924). During the Paris years, Pound even wrote an opera himself to words of François Villon, *Le Testament,* which was given only a musical performance—with the composer himself on the bass drum! It cannot have been too bad, because Virgil Thompson, who heard the performance, wrote forty years later "its sonorities are still present in my mind."

As early as 1904 Pound had begun planning the work that would occupy him for the next half-century: the epic poem *The Cantos.* The first of these was published in 1917; and, except for humorous political verse of the nineteen-thirties, they became Pound's only poetry-writing activity. And they are a colossal one. Here Pound tries to encompass our "tale of the tribe," to memorialize what he considers

most worth recording in our civilization. "It is their purpose to give the true meaning of history as one man has
found it," says the publisher's blurb for the *Rock Drill*
section.

As the 116 Cantos progress, the "one man" becomes increasingly emphasized, they become more personal and
autobiographical, and conclude with Pound himself as the
center, and the epic is Pound's life itself. The episodes are
more or less fragmentary—a feature that becomes worse as
the work continues; the increasing subjectivity is also de-
plorable. Yet one of the later groups, *The Pisan Cantos*, is
the loveliest of all, and the last two Cantos magnificently
consummate the entire poem. Pound's obsession with
money economics often bores a reader who does not share
this interest. But, taken as a whole, *The Cantos* are so rich
in perceptions of beauty and shrewd judgments of good
and evil, expressed in a pungent, vital, often very American
speech, that one can say of them, as was said of *The
Canterbury Tales:* "Here is God's plenty."

5

Retirement in Rapallo

After four years in Paris, Pound again felt that he had come to a dead end. He was weary of artistic intrigues and he needed a rest from the whirl of literary society, time for his own writing. He determined first simply to move to Italy, with no special place in mind, according to Mrs. Pound. Then an American lady friend, a writer, returned from an Italian trip. She had stayed overnight in Rapallo, a small resort town on the coast east of Genoa, and she described its charms to the Pounds. So, when they left Paris in April 1924, they made Rapallo their first stop in Italy. "It seemed pleasant enough to settle in," Dorothy Pound recalled—and after three months in Sicily they returned to live in Rapallo.

The Pounds rented an apartment on the fifth floor above a café, with a distant view of the sea—"Rapallo's thin line of broken mother-of-pearl" in Yeats' description. The apartment had a large terrace on the sea side. Most of the furniture was made by Pound himself. Rapallo was to be Pound's home for twenty years, and there he was happy. "The navel of the world," he called it; Pound had finally come home. He wrote: "London was in terror of thought.

Paris was tired, very tired. Italy was, on the other hand, full of Bounce." Only after they had settled in Rapallo did the Pounds learn that the English writer and illustrator Max Beerbohm also lived there. (He had reputedly been the model for "Brennbaum the Impeccable" in Pound's *Mauberley*.) They found him "a delightful person over tea," Mrs. Pound told me.

Desmond Chute, who then lived in Rapallo, testifies that these were paradisal years for Pound there on the Riviera di Levante, by the "green clear and blue clear" Tyrrhenian Sea. Pound was loved by the Rapallo citizenry, who universally and spontaneously called him, simply, "il poeta." Here poverty was honorable, he wrote Harriet Monroe, for a poet was respected. "He was an Ulysses seeking his island," Louise Gebhard Cann had said of him in Paris. In Rapallo he found it.

Amid the small-town surroundings, Pound was at last out of the maelstrom of literary society. His circle of writer friends was smaller, but his correspondence was enormous, his critical writing continued, *The Cantos* moved forward, and a new, much revised edition of *Personae* came out. Pound continued translations of Guido Cavalcanti, on which he had worked since before 1910, and prepared a scholarly edition of Cavalcanti, sparing no effort to make his text accurate; perhaps he was piqued by accusations that his knowledge of his translated texts was slipshod. He founded *The Exile*, which lasted through four issues in 1927 and 1928; Yeats' poem "Sailing to Byzantium" was first published in the magazine. He studied Chinese, became engrossed in Confucius, and translated that ethical philosopher. The German anthropologist Leo Frobenius, a scholar of ancient African civilization, became a new Poundian enthusiasm. In contrast to Frazer, author of *The Golden Bough*, Frobenius had *seen* what he described, Pound pointed out to me at Saint Elizabeth's. (Pound always preached firsthand examination of things rather than accepting others' opinions.)

But most important of all, he was working on *The Cantos*. Numbers 31 to 71 were composed in Rapallo— great gulps of Italian Renaissance, Chinese, and American history rendered with an astonishing liveliness. Again and again a dead man is brought to life. The past becomes contemporary. At Rapallo Pound wrote the loveliest of all the Cantos for lyric force, Canto 49, set in the seven lakes section of China:

> For the seven lakes, and by no man these verses:
> Rain; empty river; a voyage,
> Fire from frozen cloud, heavy rain in the twilight
> Under the cabin roof was one lantern.
> The reeds are heavy; bent;
> and the bamboos speak as if weeping.
>
> Autumn moon; hills rise about lakes
> against sunset
> Evening is like a curtain of cloud,
> a blurr above ripples; and through it
> sharp long spikes of the cinnamon,
> a cold tune amid reeds.
> Behind hill the monk's bell
> borne on the wind.
> Sail passed here in April; may return in October
> Boat fades in silver; slowly;
> Sun blaze alone on the river.

*   *   *

For all this serene lyric imagination, Pound was becoming more and more intransigent toward the modern world, more extreme in his demands for change. Several decades' struggle with his surroundings had taken its toll on him; his fury against modern vulgarity became giant. He wrote

Louis Zukofsky: "The period during which capitalist syfilization cd. cooperate in the ahts is evidently sinkin' to its last pozzo nero." And in *The Exile*, "Quite simply: I want a new civilization."

At Rapallo Pound read Jefferson and John Adams, and found their ideas the principles of a good society—from which, he believed, modern America had apostatized. Social Credit was still a main interest, and much of his prose writing was propaganda attacking "international finance." "A vicious economic system has corrupted every ramification of thought," he wrote. And looking back on his struggles to obtain publication of Eliot, Joyce, Lewis, Hemingway, and many others, Pound stated: "In another thirty years perhaps the gross idiocy of two decades of publishers will also be more apparent. I mean their short-sightedness; and particularly their policy of debasing the literary coin to the point where it no longer deceives even the gulls." That prediction has been fulfilled.

He wrote several retrospective autobiographical summaries, including the shocking revelation that no American publisher or "regular and established" English publisher had ever accepted a book on his recommendation, no American university or cultural institution had ever invited him to lecture, he had been invited to serve on no jury of awards in the arts, and no fellowship had ever been awarded on his recommendation. This was the fate of the most influential English language writer of our century. This is how our civilization too often makes use of its men of genius!

Two young poet disciples came to live in Rapallo, Basil Bunting and Louis Zukofsky. Bunting was an English Quaker, stubborn as Pound himself, and the Quaker moral earnestness gave the drive to his poems; Zukofsky an "objectivist" from William Carlos Williams' group who wrote with an antiseptic detachment. Pound quartered them and fed them physically as well as intellectually.

During this time, Pound's father and mother appeared in Rapallo too. Homer Pound had retired from the Mint, and one day (Dorothy Pound told me) he said to his wife with a frontiersman's directness: "We're going over to live with Ezra. We leave a month from now." So in that month Isabel Pound had to pack up the belongings of a lifetime—and somehow she did. They took an apartment near Ezra, and both ended their days in Italy. Isabel Pound kept a predilection for her son's earlier verse, which she often recited at great length, much to the poet's discomfort.

Yeats came twice to stay in Rapallo with his newlywed young wife, and an old friendship was enlivened. Pound undertook to elucidate *The Cantos'* structure to Yeats. He showed the Irish poet a photograph of a fifteenth-century mural by Cosimo Tura, in three compartments: above, the Triumphs of Love and Chastity; in the middle, zodiacal signs; beneath, certain events of Cosimo Tura's day. Pound explained that in *The Cantos* the Triumphs were replaced by archetypal persons, the civilization builders (Confucius, Sigismundo Malatesta, Thomas Jefferson), the zodiacal signs were replaced by *The Cantos'* fixed elements (descent into hell, the metamorphoses), and various modern events took the place of the events in Tura's time. At Saint Elizabeth's Pound was still using the same description; he recited it to me on one occasion.

By 1934, when Yeats returned for another visit, the friendship had cooled. Pound's violence puzzled Yeats, and his opinion of Yeats' latest drama was neither flattering nor constructive: "Putrid!" Dorothy Pound told me: "Yeats thought he would spend the evenings waving his hands at E.P. and talking, but E.P. was too busy for that."

Yet it was typical of Pound that he found more time for

promising young people than for their renowned elders. The Harvard undergraduate James Laughlin had begun to read Pound's poetry after he saw letters Pound had written his English master at Choate, Dudley Fitts. When the Dean's office gave him a year's leave of absence from college, he headed for Rapallo. There he spent the year living near Pound, lunching with the Pounds daily. The master interested him in Social Credit and incited him to launch the New Directions publishing house, which became the leading (and for several decades, the only) American avant-garde book publisher. Pound, who could never resist garbling a name for fun, was soon calling it "Nude Erections."

In the French review *L'Herne* (1965), Laughlin has left a charming memoir of those days at the "Ezuversity," as Pound called it. Laughlin had telegraphed from Paris asking if the great man could be seen. "Visibility high!" Pound wired back. "I had expected an interview; I was offered an education," writes Laughlin. The lessons of the "Ezuversity" were offered verbally as Laughlin and the Pounds strolled on the mountain paths behind Rapallo, among terraced farms and olive plantations, with that ancient sea stretched beneath them—a good place for hearing Greek and Provençal verse. Laughlin testifies that the master's tennis forehand was formidable, and he was thoroughly enjoying himself in Rapallo:

> After dinner he often went to the local cinema and sat in the front row of the balcony, his feet on the railing. The Italian film industry was then still far from having any artistic pretensions; I could never understand how he could endure these comedies, but he seemed to find them very funny.

Pound also busied himself with organizing concerts of ancient music at the Rapallo town hall. At Saint Elizabeth's

he declared with pride that he had converted the inhabitants of Rapallo from Verdi to Vivaldi. Whether the con-
version was lasting or not, those Rapallo concerts were a
monument to Pound's enthusiasm and enterprise. The only
help received from the city authorities was the loan of the
hall. Pound insisted on having "blocks" of music: all the
Mozart violin and piano sonatas played on successive days
by Olga Rudge and Gerhart Münch, then all Bach's violin
sonatas and all Pergolesi's. On three consecutive after-
noons, Münch performed the complete *Wohltemperierte
Klavier*. The seventeenth-century English composers Pur-
cell and William Young were stressed. Some Vivaldi *in-
edita* were given their first performance, and Münch played
his transcriptions of Dowland, Jannequin, and Francesco
da Milano. The Hungarian Quartet performed Bartók, at
that time rarely played and little known, and Hindemith
was heard. Pound's Rapallo concerts were at least a decade
in advance of his time. Now the early music which he emphasized in these concerts is much more widely appreciated.

During the mid-thirties, Pound's advice was sought by
two translators, W. H. D. Rouse, who was doing *The
Odyssey*, and Lawrence Binyon, making an English version
of *The Divine Comedy*. Pound went over their manuscripts line by line, and both profited by his suggestions.
But economic matters occupied more and more of his attention. He writes in *ABC of Reading* (1934): "The chief
cause of false writing is economic. Many writers need or
want money. These writers could be cured by an application of banknotes." It was as simple as that. Writers need
money. Give it to them—paper money; then they would
write well, Pound was saying. Pound himself, as one of the
world's best-known writers, still had an income of less than
$500 a year from his homeland.

He became more and more partisan to Mussolini, who

had ruled Italy since 1922. In *Jefferson and/or Mussolini* (1935), he eulogized "the Boss," declaring that Mussolini was no despot but an establisher of order and honest government. The Italian invasion of Ethiopia and the alliance with Hitler failed to change his mind. War tensions in Europe increased—to Pound's intense distress. He believed international bankers were responsible, especially Jewish ones. Pound had always favored the Hellenic elements of our civilization against the Hebrew; now he became fervid in his bias against Jewish cultural and financial influences, real and imagined. Yet he was still without personal prejudices, as witness his inexhaustible kindness to Louis Zukofsky during these times; Zukofsky was a Jew of leftist political views. Pound's last book of literary criticism, *Guide to Kulchur* (1938), is dedicated to Zukofsky and Basil Bunting.

By the late thirties Europe was wracked with anxiety over the oncoming war, and Pound seems to have caught the hysteria. A sensitively social person, he felt the impending tragedy as few other poets did, and he lost all balance and measure. Unfortunately, he was already on the wrong track for stopping the war. His economic ideas became an obsession. He addressed "stop the war" letters to most of the European heads of state. He wrote *Twentieth Century Authors*, which had sent a routine request for biographical information: "If you can't print my one page 'Introductory Text Book' [on economics] enclosed . . . then your profession of wanting an authentic record is mere bunk, and fit only to stand with the infamies that have raged in America since Johnson was kicked out of the White House." Andrew Johnson was of course not kicked out of the White House—an astonishing error for a longtime student of American history—and the tone of the whole letter indicates something more than a slip of the pen: a disturbance of the mental faculty through frenzy.

6

Rome Radio

Then, as Pound writes in an autobiographical sketch, "1939 first visit to U.S. since 1910 in endeavour to stave off war." He went back to Hamilton College, where he received an honorary doctorate, long overdue academic balm for this irritable poet. The citation presents the unusual spectacle of Pound, the most unacademic of persons, being generously and understandingly regarded by an academic institution. If he had always received this kind of recognition from society, he might not have gone as far off the track as he did. The citation ended:

> . . . . Your reputation is international, you have guided many poets into new paths, you have pointed new directions, and the historian of the future in tracing the development of your growing mind will inevitably, we are happy to think, be led to Hamilton and to the influence of your college teachers. You have ever been a generous champion of younger writers as well as of artists in other fields, and for this fine and rare human quality and for your own achievements in poetry and prose, we honor you.

The main speaker at the Hamilton commencement exercises was the radio commentator H. V. Kaltenborn, who defended democracy in a platitudinous oration. Pound rather boorishly heckled him while he spoke, and the two men became very angry at each other.

But "staving off war" was what brought Pound back to the States. He visited Harvard, where he wanted most to talk with members of the Economics Department, and argued with government leaders in Washington. As might have been expected, there was little communication, and he returned to Italy.

Whereupon, according to Pound:

> 1940 after continued opposition obtained permission to use Rome radio for personal propaganda in support of U.S. Constitution, continuing after America's official entry into the war only on condition that he should never be asked to say anything contrary to his conscience or contrary to his duties as an American citizen. Which promise was faithfully observed by the Italian government.

In this statement the word *personal* should be emphasized. Pound was no "Tokyo Rose" or "Lord Haw-Haw" making propaganda to break the troops' morale; most of his short-wave broadcasts to America were so idiosyncratic they could hardly have corrupted the troops, even if he had wanted that. The broadcasts expounded his views about the evil workings of "usury," and the Jewish obsession was a frequent and ugly theme. Though Hitler and Mussolini were obviously the aggressors—at the very least in a technical sense—he refused to believe they had *caused* the war. The broadcasts were certainly composed in a kind of frenzy; on July 6, 1942, we find him saying: "I am enraged by the delay needed to change the typing ribbon, so much is there that ought to be put in young America's head." Pound received 350 lire for scripts that he wrote and broadcast, and 300 for scripts he wrote for other broadcasters. Since his royalties from America and England were cut off by the war, he had no other source of income. Pound spoke twice a week on Rome Radio from January 1941 until July 1943. Only after Pearl Harbor, when the broadcasts became possibly treasonable, were they monitored and transcribed by the Federal Communications Commission in Washington.

Pound seems to have had little sense of his audience in those Rome Radio talks. As T. S. Eliot once said of him, he did not explain his economic theories, but spoke as if his listeners were already acquainted with those theories and somehow did not understand them. He raged against the war, "the usury system," President Franklin Roosevelt, and "the big Jews." He attacked the Talmud and the Old Testament. He declared the Protocols of Zion essential reading. He lambasted "usury" for impoverishing the farmers of India. He said the war was destroying American liberty; it was caused by a few international financiers. He advocated "Mediterranean sanity" as against decadence in art. He predicted that World War Two was building up toward a war between the United States and Russia; this war too was undesirable, he said. He damned Archibald MacLeish, Churchill, Morgenthau, Baruch, the American "melting pot." He questioned Roosevelt's sanity, blamed him for bringing America into the war. He declared himself the heir of his grandfather's ideas on finance (nineteenth-century populism, silver as against gold, the Bryan movement). He even blamed "New York Jew millionaires for creating Bolshevism! He discussed Confucius, Joyce, Brooks Adams (who wrote history of finance), T. S. Eliot, Cummings, Henry James, modern painting. He rambled from subject to subject, presenting a whole almanac of his views on almost everything.

Much of the broadcasts is so fanatic that they are a disgrace to him. Now and then there is perception, but fury disfigures the whole. Pound's fixation (Marianne Moore's word) on Jews and international banking is a sad thing. One surmises that Pound was partly swung by the times. Though his ideas had been brewing for twenty years, there was surely a great increase in his prejudices from 1938 to 1940, just when Mussolini was introducing anti-Jewish laws. The Pound of the broadcasts is the same man who only a few years before had dedicated his last critical book to the Jew Louis Zukofsky!

However, we must concede that the broadcasts were done out of conviction and at some risk to his life. Pound regarded himself a loyal American, so he declined to renounce his U.S. citizenship, as did other Americans who stayed in Italy and supported the Fascist government. Had he become an Italian citizen, he could not later have been prosecuted for treason. The Mussolini government gave him no special treatment because of the broadcasts. "From his mode of life it was evident that he did not enjoy privileges, but that he even suffered hardships and privations," sixty of his Rapallo neighbors later testified in a petition. Dorothy Pound described how she had to cook sea water to get a very distasteful salt for their food.

From various sources (Pound himself would not discuss it), we learn that in 1941 the Pounds disposed of all their belongings in Rapallo and tried to return to the United States on the last diplomatic train taking American citizens from Rome to Lisbon. But a consular official denied them permission to board the train, presumably on the grounds that Pound was known as a Mussolini supporter. So the die was cast, and when Pound continued his broadcasts after December 1941, he was now in the position of "giving aid and comfort to the enemy."

In July 1943, a District of Columbia grand jury indicted

Pound for treason. On learning of the indictment, Pound wrote United States Attorney General Francis Biddle, mixing reasonable argument with ranting:

> I understand that I am under indictment for treason. I have done my best to get an authentic report of your statement to this effect. And I wish to place the following facts before you.
>
> I do not believe that the simple fact of speaking over the radio, wherever placed, can in itself constitute treason. I think this must depend on what is said, and on the motives for speaking.
>
> I obtained the concession to speak over Rome radio with the following proviso. Namely that nothing should be asked of me contrary to my conscience or contrary to my duties as an American citizen. I obtained a declaration on their part of a belief in "the free expression of opinion by those qualified to have an opinion."
>
> The legal mind of the Attorney General will understand the interest inherent in this distinction, as from unqualified right of expression.
>
> This declaration was made several times in the announcement of my speeches; with the declaration "He will not be asked to say anything contrary to his conscience, or contrary to his duties as an American citizen" (Citizen of the U.S.).
>
> These conditions have been adhered to. The only time I had an opinion as to what might be interesting as subject matter, I was asked whether I would speak of religion. This seemed to me hardly my subject, though I did transmit on one occasion some passages of Confucius, under the title "The Organum of Confucius."
>
> I have not spoken with regard to *this* war, but in protest against a system which creates one war after another, in series and in system. I have not spoken to the troops, and have not suggested that the troops should mutiny or revolt. The whole basis of democratic or

majority government assumes that the citizen should be informed of the facts. I have not claimed to know all the facts, but I have claimed to know some of the facts which are an essential part of the total that should be known to the people.

I have for years believed that the American people should be better informed as to Europe, and informed by men who are not tied to a special interest or under definite control.

The freedom of the press has become a farce, as everyone knows that the press is controlled, if not by its titular owners, at least by the advertisers.

Free speech under modern conditions becomes a mockery if it do not include the right to free speech over the radio.

And this point is worth establishing. The assumption of the right to punish and take vengeance regardless of the area of jurisdiction is dangerous. I do not mean in a small way; but for the nation.

I returned to America before the war to protest against particular forces then engaged in trying to create war and to make sure that the U.S.A. should be dragged into it.

Arthur Kitson's testimony before the Cunliffe and Macmillan commissions was insufficiently known. Brooks Adams brought to light several currents in history that should be better known. The course of events following the foundation of the Bank of England should be known, and considered in sequence; the suppression of colonial paper money, especially in Pennsylvania! The similar curves following the Napoleonic Wars, and our Civil War and Versailles need more attention.

We have not the right to drift into another error similar to that of the Versailles Treaty.

We have, I think, the right to a moderate expansion including defense of the Caribbean, the elimination of foreign powers from the American continent, but such expansion should not take place at the cost of deteriorating or ruining the internal structure of the U.S.A. The ruin of markets, the perversions of trade routes, in fact all the matters on which my talks have been based is of importance to the American citizen; [whom] neither you nor I should betray either in time of war *or* peace. I may say in passing that I took out a life membership in the American Academy of Social and Political Science in the hope of obtaining fuller discussion of some of these issues, but did not find them ready for full and frank expression of certain vital elements in the case, this may in part have been due to their incomprehension of the nature of the case.

At any rate a man's duties increase with his knowledge. A war between the U.S. and Italy is monstrous and should not have occurred. And a peace without justice is no peace but merely a prelude to future wars. Someone must take count of these things. And having taken count must act on his knowledge; admitting that his knowledge is partial and his judgment subject to error.

Pound's broadcasts ended in 1943, when the Mussolini regime was overthrown and replaced by a provisional government. Rome was in chaos, so the fifty-eight-year-old poet borrowed a knapsack, a map, and a pair of walking boots and set out northward. He hiked six hundred miles, sleeping in farms and dormitories and in the open, receiving food from kindly women, till he arrived in the South Tyrolean village of Gais, where his teen-age daughter was being kept by a peasant lady. Snatches of conversation in Canto 78 of *The Pisan Cantos* tells the story:

> the man out of Naxos past Fara Sabina
> "if you will stay for the night"
> "it is true there is only one room for the lot of us"

"money is nothing"
"no, there is nothing to pay for that bread"

* * *

"Nothing left here but women"

* * *

No, they will do nothing to you.
"Who *says* he is an American"

And, with impeccable memory for Tyrolean speech, he records his arrival in Gais, his feet all blisters:

"Grüss Gott," "Derr Herr!" "Tatile ist gekommen!"

("Good afternoon," "The master!" "Papa has come!") After a few weeks with his daughter, he went down to join Dorothy Pound and Olga Rudge in Rapallo.

During the war years Pound wrote little poetry. The two Cantos (72 and 73) composed in these times were mainly in Italian and about his economic ideas. Curiously enough, he never allowed them to be published, and today in both American and British editions of *The Cantos* there is a gap between Cantos 71 and 74.

Late in the war, when the Germans fortified the Rapallo waterfront area, the Pounds were thrown out of their apartment. They went to live with Olga Rudge in the hills above Rapallo. Then on May 5, 1945, Dorothy Pound came back from an attempt to get food in Rapallo and found—no Ezra. Two Italian partisans had taken him away and turned him over to the American army. Interviewed by a reporter at this time, he said: "If a man isn't willing to take some risks for his opinions, either his opinions are no good or he's no good."

Pound was shipped to a "Disciplinary Training Center" in Pisa, a special stockade for the worst U.S. Army criminals, where he was the only civilian prisoner. He was confined in a grilled security cage (the "gorilla cage" of *The Cantos*), one of a line of cages in the "death row" for men awaiting execution. There was little shelter from sun and rain; the cage had only a tarpaper roof. Searchlights lit up the cage all night. Two guards stood watch twenty-four hours round. Pound slept on the cement floor with six blankets. Dust from a nearby highway inflamed his eyes. He could speak to no one, and was told no one knew where he was. After three weeks of this barbarous mistreatment, he suffered a breakdown.

He was transferred to a tent within the medical compound, where he remained for five more months. Furniture was one cot and a box ("that bacon box . . . now used as a wardrobe"); later he obtained a second cot and a table. For books he had a Bible and his Legge edition of Confucius, the Chinese text with an English translation. And now, awaiting a trial that could cost his life, Pound composed one of *The Cantos'* enduring sections, the so-called *Pisan Cantos*, superbly cadenced verse that shows a marvelous sensitivity, much wisdom, even good humor, and—implicit in all, considering the circumstances of its composition—courage and a profound sorrow. Hemingway told Douglass Paige he considered it Pound's finest poetry.

> till the shrine be again white with marble
> till the stone eyes look again seaward
> The wind is part of the process
> The rain is part of the process
> and the Pleiades set in her mirror
> *   *   *
> Time is not, Time is the evil, beloved
> Beloved the hours *brododaktulos*
> as against the half-light of the window
> with the sea beyond making horizon
> le contre-jour the line of the cameo
> profile "to carve Achaia"
> a dream passing over the face in the half-light

At Saint Elizabeth's Pound described to me how he would compose *The Pisan Cantos* in his head during the day, then in the evening go to the dispensary, where the medics allowed him to use a typewriter, and type out the day's work.

On October 3 (after five months of confinement) he was allowed his first visitor, his wife. Mrs. Pound told me that she had been informed absolutely nothing about her husband during these five months. She did not even know whether he was alive. Finally she received a letter from an American general: "If you wish to see your husband . . ." Arriving at the Pisa stockade, she asked for her husband with some trepidation, hardly knowing what to expect. Whereupon a G.I. bellowed out: "TELL UNCLE EZRA HIS WIFE IS HERE!"

The autumn rains began, and Pound's tent was hardly comfortable. His request for more blankets was delayed for a week by a bureaucratic corporal. Passages in the last two *Pisan Cantos* give a hint of how the sixty-year-old poet fared as the weather grew colder

> in the drenched tent there is quiet
> sered eyes are at rest

and *The Pisan Cantos'* concluding lines

> If the hoar frost grip thy tent
> Thou wilt give thanks when night is spent.

During the whole six months at Pisa, he was not permitted to send or receive letters. Mrs. Pound was allowed to visit him once more, and his daughter came once.

A guard at Pisa, Robert L. Allen, has described Pound's last evening in the detention camp. The poet sat in the dispensary reading Joseph E. Davies' *Mission to Moscow*, with the Charge of Quarters at the desk beside him; from time to time he would make a comment to the C.Q. Suddenly the door was flung open and two lieutenants entered. Pound should be ready to leave for Washington within an hour, they said, then turned on their heels and departed. The poet handed the book to the C.Q. and asked him to thank all the medics for him. As he reached the door of the barracks he turned about with a half smile, put both hands round his neck like a noose, and jerked his chin up.

Pound's mistreatment at Pisa clearly violated various provisions of the United States Constitution—as indicated by Professor Giovanni Giovannini of the Catholic University of America (statement entered in the *Congressional Record,* May 6, 1958, by Representative Usher L. Burdick). Amendment VIII forbids "cruel and unusual punishment"; confining an elderly man in an open cage is just this. And Professor Giovannini says

> Detaining a civilian prisoner for so long a time as 6 months without arraignment, access to counsel, right of bail, and a speedy trial appear as violation of clauses in the Constitution:
>
> 1. Amendment V which assures citizens the right not to be deprived of liberty "without due process of law."
>
> 2. Amendment VI which states that "in all criminal prosecutions, the accused shall enjoy the right to a speedy and public trial" and "have the assistance of counsel."
>
> 3. Article I, section 9, which states that "the privilege of the writ of habeas corpus shall not be suspended, unless when in cases of rebellion or invasion the public safety may require it."
>
> There was neither rebellion nor invasion of the United States between May and November of 1945 (the war in fact had ended in all theaters by September), but during this time the authorities in Pound's case in effect suspended the writ.

Who *were* the authorities in Pound's case? At Saint Elizabeth's Pound was convinced that his treatment in Pisa had been ordered directly from the White House. But I suspect President Truman himself had as little control over Pound's mishandling as he did over the decision to drop the atom bombs at Hiroshima and Nagasaki.

On November 18, 1945, Pound was flown to Washington, D.C., and there reindicted:

> Ezra Pound . . . a citizen of the United States of America and a person owing allegiance to the United States of America . . . at Rome, Italy, and other places within the Kingdom of Italy . . . in violation of his duty of allegiance, knowingly, intentionally, willfully, unlawfully, feloniously, traitorously and treasonably did adhere to the enemies of the United States, to wit: the Kingdom of Italy and the military allies of the said Kingdom of Italy, with which the United States at all times since December 11, 1941 . . . have been at war, giving to the said enemies of the United States aid and comfort within the United States and elsewhere. . . .

While being held at District Jail in Washington, Pound declared his intention of subpoenaing for his defense Henry Wallace, then Secretary of Agriculture, and Archibald MacLeish, Assistant Secretary of State, both of whom he had seen in his 1939 visit to America. He asked for and received a Georgian grammar at the jail; he wanted to learn Georgian in order to convert Stalin to his economic ideas!

Pound was arraigned the day after his arrival in Washington, and asked for permission to act as his own counsel, but the judge told him the charge was too serious for that. So Julian Cornell, a friend of James Laughlin, was retained as counsel. Pound stood mute on formal arraignment eight days later, and a plea of innocence was entered by Cornell, who declared that "Mr. Pound is not sufficiently in possession of judgment and perhaps mentality to plead," and requested that Pound be examined for sanity. And the court so ordered. Pound declined to ask for bail, telling his lawyer his total resources were twenty-three dollars. E. E. Cummings had just sold one of his paintings for a thousand dollars, and he immediately sent the money on to Pound as a gift. James Laughlin contributed two hundred dollars, and Archibald MacLeish forwarded fifty dollars a lady had sent him for Pound.

Robert Graves' contribution to letters at this time was to urge publicly that Pound be hung.

At Gallinger Hospital Pound was examined by four psychiatrists, who reported him insane:

> The undersigned hereby respectfully report on the results of their mental examination of Ezra Pound, now detained in Gallinger Hospital by transfer for observation from the District Jail on a charge of treason. Three of us (Drs. Gilbert, King and Overholser) were appointed by your Honor to make this examination. At our suggestion, and with your approval, Dr. Wendell Muncie, acting upon request of counsel for the accused, made an examination with us and associates himself with us in this joint report. Dr. Muncie spent several hours with the defendant, both alone and with us, on December 13, 1945, and others of us have examined the defendant each on several occasions, separately and together, in the period from his admission to Gallinger Hospital on December 4, 1945, to December 13, 1945. We have had available to us reports of laboratory, psychological and special physical examinations of the defendant and considerable material in the line of his writings and biographical data.
>
> The defendant, now sixty years of age and in generally good physical condition, was a precocious student, specializing in literature. He has been a voluntary ex-

patriate for nearly forty years, living in England and France, and for the past twenty-one years in Italy, making an uncertain living by writing poetry and criticism. His poetry and literary criticism have achieved considerable recognition, but of recent years his preoccupation with monetary theories and economics has apparently obstructed his literary productivity. He has long been recognized as eccentric, querulous and egocentric.

At the present time he exhibits extremely poor judgment as to his situation, its seriousness and the manner in which the charges are to be met. He insists that the broadcasts were not treasonable, but that all his radio activities have stemmed from his self appointed mission to "save the Constitution." He is abnormally grandiose, is expansive and exuberant in manner, exhibiting pressure of speech, discursiveness, and distractibility.

In our opinion, with advancing years his personality, for many years abnormal, has undergone further distortion to the extent that he is now suffering from a paranoid state which renders him mentally unfit to advise properly with counsel or to participate intelligently and reasonably in his defense. He is, in other words, insane and mentally unfit for trial, and is in need of care in a mental hospital.

One sentence in the psychiatrists' report—"He has been a voluntary expatriate for nearly forty years . . . making an uncertain living by writing poetry and criticism"—calls to mind the responsibility of all our society for what Pound did on Rome Radio. Anyone who has not himself made an uncertain living for forty years—often hardly knowing where the next meal is coming from—need only try to imagine the effect of that situation, continuing for forty years, on the mind and attitudes of the person suffering it. And if a society accords this treatment to its greatest poet . . . ? Is there really any excuse for what our society did to Ezra Pound?

Lawyers for the United States government asked that a jury be empaneled to pass on the psychiatrists' report. This was done, and at a sanity hearing on February 13, 1946, the examining psychiatrists testified to the Court that Pound was mentally unfit to stand trial. Dr. Marion King, medical director of the U.S. Public Health Service, stated that he considered Pound a "sensitive, eccentric, cynical person" who was in "a paranoic state of psychotic proportions which renders him unfit for trial." The judge closed his instructions to the jury:

> It therefore becomes your duty now to advise me whether in your judgment you find that Mr. Pound is in position to cooperate with his counsel, to stand trial without causing him to crack up or break down, whether he is able to testify, if he sees fit, at the trial, to stand cross-examination, and in that regard, of course, you have heard the testimony of all these physicians on the subject, and there is no testimony to the contrary and, of course, these are men who have given a large part of their professional careers to the study of matters of this sort, who have been brought here for your guidance.
>
> Under the state of the law you are not necessarily bound by what they say; you can disregard what they say and bring in a different verdict, but in a case of this type where the Government and the defense representatives have united in a clear and unequivocal view with regard to the situation, I presume you will have no difficulty in making up your mind.

And the jury declared Pound "of unsound mind."

After this verdict Pound was "committed to the custody of the United States" and sent to Saint Elizabeth's Hospital in Washington, this being the only federal government insane asylum. All persons accused of a federal crime and found insane must be confined there.

It may be thought that Pound got off lightly. After all, he could have been imprisoned or even executed. However, aside from the fact that some clemency might have been expected for a great poet, it is by no means sure that the government could have obtained a conviction. The Supreme Court had already ruled in the case of *Cramer v. United States* that there is no treason without treasonable intent. The net effect of the psychiatrists' report was that Pound was incarcerated for thirteen years without being convicted of a crime.

At Saint Elizabeth's he was first placed in a windowless criminal lunatic ward, Howard Hall, where every other inmate was in a strait-jacket. For a year and a half he literally saw no daylight. He was allowed to receive visitors for fifteen minutes in the presence of a guard. His wife could not visit him for several years; she still remained in Italy, because the U.S. State Department held up her request for a visa.

Finally Pound was transferred to a regular ward in Center Building. Here visitors were permitted two hours daily. He had a tiny private room with a dressing table, a bed, and a high narrow window of leaded glass covered by grillwork. His cubicle was doorless. Hence for all the years at Saint Elizabeth's he was never alone.

Thus fate swept into Washington a man who perhaps more than anyone else had shaped twentieth-century English literature. The circumstances were dirty and unpleasant. For all that, his personal integrity was uncompromised, and the history of what he had done for writing in our time remained. W. H. Auden wrote: "There are very few living poets, even if they are not conscious of having been influenced by Pound, who could say, 'My work would be exactly the same if Mr. Pound had never lived.' "

In fact, all of us today probably think differently than we would if Pound had not fought his life's fight. And if we blame Pound for belligerence and some fantastic views, we should not forget that he had an uphill struggle all the way. His poetic and critical victories were won despite fierce opposition, and he usually had just enough funds to survive (while men parasitic on him, he noted with acerbity, received fat grants). "Now if ever it is time to cleanse Helicon," he wrote in *Homage to Sextus Propertius*. And he undertook the Herculean task.

PART TWO

Mr. Pound's Elizabethan Age

I

Saint Elizabeth's

That place, beginning with its great red-brick front gate, is a lesson in ugliness. The massive brick hospital buildings remind one of Mencken's dissertation on the American "libido for the ugly." Such horrors could not happen by chance, nor could mere ignorance explain them. Only a positive love of ugliness could have inspired their creation.

Yet the grounds themselves are pleasantly wooded. When you first spy the elms towering above the outside wall, you take a deep breath, for this is healthy compared to what you have just passed through. To reach the hospital, you board a bus among the Pennsylvania Avenue government buildings, Washington's claim to splendor, which careens along the right side of the Capitol building, then through Negro slums, past gas-storage depots, over a branch of the Potomac, and into a wilderness of dingy row houses in southeast Washington. Finally the brick wall of Saint Elizabeth's appears on the right.

The hospital sprawls over many acres, so that a walk from the main gate to the Superintendent's office—which I undertook on my first visit—is quite a hike. Asphalt driveways connect the buildings. During spring and summer, greenery is everywhere.

If you visit in the summertime, you walk among tall clumps of boxwood after entering the front gate, then emerge on an expanse of lawn. Here and there, men drift about or sit on benches, dumbly staring: inmates. About seventy-five yards off, dwarfed beneath the great elms, a small group sits on garden chairs. You approach, and discern a broad-shouldered gentleman with a tangly gray beard reclining very low on a long camp chair, his face seamed, cheeks and forehead high with age. He offers his hand wordlessly, leaning forward on his chair. His eyes, green behind many wrinkles, are quick. This is Ezra Pound.

To his left sits his wife Dorothy—gray, spare, and dignified—a cameo still, and once surely more beautiful. Her clipped speech has a British resonance, her manner a British restraint. There may be no other visitors, or as many as seven or eight: disciples (some bearded in imitation of the master), literary people, professors, Social Creditors, and a variety of other strange personages. Conversation of course centers in Mr. Pound. He is allowed the freedom of the grounds in front of his ward, and exercises this privilege in good weather. Visiting hours are from two to four daily, and Dorothy Pound appears promptly at two.

Greetings done, you walk to the office of Center Building, at the end of the lawn, where visitors must check in. At the office a white-coated attendant asks your name and consults a card file. Then you return to the little group under the elms.

In winter, things are quite different. First you stop by the office. After the whitecoat grunts his approval, you emerge into the cold again, walk a few chilly steps, and duck into an entranceway that leads to a long spiral metal staircase. Though Pound's ward is in the same building as the office, there seems to be no direct communication—for security reasons, perhaps. At the top of the stairs is a door massive as a bank vault's. You press a button, and eventually a whitecoat opens from inside. The great door swings in, admitting you to a hallway peopled by the derelicts of Saint Elizabeth's, some in bathrobe, others fully dressed. They mutter to themselves and stare; some drool; some make short senseless motions with their hands. A few watch television. The door clangs shut behind you. You walk down the hallway, turn left, and there, in an alcove by a window, sit Pound and his visitors. A movable screen separates them from the sullen, silent bedlam.

Mr. Pound is tolerant and kindly with his fellow inmates. When one drifts past the screen, the poet gently guides him off. Another gets a penny placed in his hand. Pound has even become friendly with some of them. One is there, Pound explains jovially, because he prefers being locked up to paying alimony. Though Pound jokes about his incarceration—calls Saint Elizabeth's "the bug-house"—it must gnaw. The surroundings are thoroughly humiliating for a sensitive and cultured gentleman. They must increase his already large resentment against the order of society.

There, by the window opening on a wintry landscape, the steam radiator sings and Mr. Pound's voice runs on. His talk is the liveliest I have ever heard, sometimes even boisterously good-humored, but sadness seems underneath it all. A host of friends are dead. He is accused of treason, has never been tried. There is no way of knowing if he will ever see his loved places again. An old man and his memories.

2

Where the Dead Walked

in meine Heimat
          where the dead walked
       and the living were made of cardboard

he wrote in Canto 115.

In his homeland, at Saint Elizabeth's, memories were the main topic of Mr. Pound's conversation. However, I thought he did not deliberately live in the past. After all, the hospital environment was extremely restricted, and hardly stimulating. Visitors appeared only two hours daily, and these were not always the liveliest conversationalists. So he had little choice but to dip into memory.

What events did occur in his very limited ambiance seemed to interest him, and he received visitors with great pleasure. To those who came he was invariably helpful and gracious. I remember him once amiably urging me to stay when I was about to leave with the other visitors before the two hours were up. Yet he talked often of those memories that haunt his later verse—summarized by a paraphrase of Anglo-Saxon poetry in *The Pisan Cantos:*

Lordly men are to earth o'ergiven

Pound's mind was selective rather than encyclopedic, so the colorful and funny stories were the ones he remembered. He loved mimicry, and was very good at it. I mentioned to him my difficulty finding books in the Paris Bibliothèque Nationale. He replied with a story from three decades earlier, when he had approached an official at the same institution with the same complaint. "Monsieur, votre catalogue est une *BLAGUE!* [Your catalogue is a *joke!*]," Mr. Pound had roared. Then he imitated sputtering red-faced bureaucratic indignation as the official repeats incredulously: "*Blague?* Monsieur dit . . . que notre catalogue . . . est une . . . une . . . *blague.* . . ?"

The Cantos are often a highly refined representation of Pound's own talk. Their tone is basically conversational, which makes them lively and real. Such poetry convinces us that we ourselves could have thought it, said T. S. Eliot. It runs in our head as naturally as our own thoughts.

But when Pound related an anecdote from *The Cantos* in person, it was even more vivid than on the page. Once I informed him that I was contemplating teaching at Harvard, where I was then a graduate student. Whereupon he related a story which is in Canto 84, told him by George Santayana. The young Santayana informs a very aged Henry Adams that he plans to teach at Harvard. Pound imitates Adams' Boston drawl and the palsied head-shaking of an old man as he tells Adams' answer: "Teach . . . at *Hah-vahd?* Teach [three-second pause] at *HAAH-VAHD??* [Three seconds more.] It . . . [three seconds] . . . cahn't . . . [five seconds—vigorous cranial trembling] . . . be done."

At Saint Elizabeth's memories of old friends often appeared as anecdotes. "Yeats," said Pound unceremoniously, "believed in spooks." And he told how Yeats sometimes fancied himself to be receiving messages from the spirit world. He and Yeats were seated at an outdoor café in Rapallo when a highly scented lady of pleasure strolled by. "An odor from another world!" announced Yeats, who had not noticed the very this-worldly lady.

Pound also described Yeats' reaction when, about 1915, Carl Jung's ideas hit London in the form of a vigorously proselytizing female who spread the gospel through the literary salons. Said Yeats (Pound burlesquing his brogue): "Most a*MA*zingly pure-minded young woman I've ever met. Why, she spoke of a phallus as if it were a mere . . . a mere . . . *CAR*-rot!"

(Pound was dead set against all psychiatry—when asked whether Jung or Freud was better, said he couldn't distinguish between contents of the sewer. For years, the Saint Elizabeth's doctors urged him to submit to psychoanalysis —in vain, of course.)

T. S. Eliot visited Pound at Saint Elizabeth's when his lectures and verse readings brought him to America. Pound spoke of Eliot with esteem, though their friendship had perhaps cooled since the days they edited *The Egoist* together in a London basement and addressed each other in Uncle Remus language, for fun. This, Pound said at Saint Elizabeth's, was the origin of Eliot's nickname "Old Possum." Now Eliot was a kind of literary saint for England, and a lot of water had gone over the dam. The two men had diverged intellectually—Eliot toward the high Anglican Church, Pound toward money economics. I heard Pound grumbling that while his friend Henry Swabey had translated Lancelot Andrewes' Latin tracts against usury, Eliot had been interested only in Andrewes' sermons.

Nevertheless, Pound always cherished old friends especially, and a warmth for Eliot seemed to be there. About his conversations with Eliot at Saint Elizabeth's, he said, "There is always a core of solid sense in Mr. Eliot's talk."

(In general he found Eliot too diffuse—but he prized the core.) And he enjoyed mischievously telling a story from his London days: the very conscientious Mr. Eliot opened the wrong door in his rooming house and found himself in his landlady's bedroom, then had much ado persuading his wife that it was "quite by error, dear, *quite* by error."

Pound did not like to talk about James Joyce; I believe the reasons were personal as well as literary. Joyce lived in a Joyce-centered universe, and I had the impression that Pound considered the Irish writer insufficiently grateful for the help Pound had given him. Moreover, after Harriet Weaver had set Joyce up, he lived in considerable style in a Paris apartment, and Pound seems to have felt that his money might have been better spent—perhaps on helping other writers, as Pound himself did. And most important, Pound thought that Joyce's literary influence was bad. He called *Finnegan's Wake* "that diarrhoea of consciousness." "Hemingway had sense enough to see that *Ulysses* was the end and not a beginning," he told D. G. Bridson—that is, Hemingway knew Joyce was not to be imitated. Maybe Pound was even a bit envious of Joyce's influence and reputation.

What was Joyce like in person? At Saint Elizabeth's Pound would speak only of Joyce's heavy drinking. "Nobody is entertaining when stiff," he said dryly. Then he recalled a drunken Joyce in Paris trying to kick the chandelier. On another occasion Pound declared that Joyce was anti-Semitic (I believe I had just accused him of being so himself), and cited as evidence the scene in *Ulysses* where Leopold Bloom flies up to heaven as the Prophet Elijah!

Pound's dislike of *Finnegan's Wake's* "circumambient periphrasation"—as he called it in a letter to Joyce—seems to have become retroactive to *Ulysses*. When visitors would mention *Ulysses* at Saint Elizabeth's (perhaps thinking this would please the man who had been instrumental in getting it published), Pound would immediately praise another work of eccentric sentence structure, E. E. Cummings' Russian travel journal *Eimi*, and suggest reading *Eimi* instead. The comparison seemed to me irrelevant, as the two books are only superficially similar.

Pound spoke affectionately of Ernest Hemingway, whom he called "Hem." Once, to tease him, I suggested he get in on the lucrative beer-endorsement business, and gave him a Rheingold beer ad that I had torn from a magazine. A photo showed Hemingway sitting in shorts amid tropical surroundings—burly, hairy, and content—holding, of course, a glass of Rheingold. Pound instantly folded part of the ad over, and handed it back to me, a mischievous glimmer in his eye. Now you saw only Hemingway in shorts and the big black print of the slogan: PURITY—BODY—FLAVOR.

Hemingway did not visit Pound at Saint Elizabeth's. Douglass Paige, editor of Pound's *Letters,* wrote me about a rather strange talk with Hemingway at Rapallo in 1949, where that great stylist tried to explain why he did not go to see Pound:

> I told him that E. P. complained about a lack of visitors. Hemingway replied, "He's lucky!" and went on to say that a writer had to be left alone to write; visitors distracted him from his work. I said that was fine for many writers, but that Ezra was a catalyst of persons and the reactions that he brought about fed his creative juices.
>
> A little later I wondered aloud if anything could be done to liberate E. P., and if he, Eliot, Mencken, etc., got together. . . . Hemingway interrupted to say vehemently that he thought there could be no worse idea than trying to interfere. He told about a Colonel or General in the Tank Corps whose son had been cap-

tured by the retreating Germans. This officer, instead of letting things go (the Germans themselves were surrounded in the meantime by the Maquis), ordered an all-out attack. The fighting was very bitter, and in the course of it the son was killed. Had the officer been patient, the Germans would have surrendered to the Maquis, together with their prisoners.

Hemingway felt that the visits of Mencken, Eliot and other well-known people only made the situation more difficult, for the visits were publicized and the "opposition" only dug itself in the more. Publicity was the worst thing; it got Ezra into trouble in the first place. No one was paying any attention to the broadcasts, and then MacLeish got upset and rushed to Washington to see if somehow E. P. could be shielded from a treason charge. He raised such a fuss that the Administration was then forced to have the Dept. of Justice draw up a True Bill.—Such was Hemingway's story.

Hemingway's argument seems eccentric. Paige thought he felt guilty about not visiting Pound. One wonders what his real reasons were. Politics? In his Paris memoirs, Hemingway wrote of Pound: "His own writing, when he would hit it right, was so perfect, and he was so sincere in his mistakes and so enamored of his errors, and so kind to people that I always thought of him as a sort of saint. He was also irascible but so perhaps have been many saints." So it would appear that Hemingway's admiration and affection for Pound had not diminished. I think that Hemingway's failure to go out to Saint Elizabeth's had to do with some personal quirk of his. Perhaps visiting a crazy house did not fit the he-man world-sportsman role in which Hemingway (often much to his own discomfort) had cast himself.

The two writers had not met since 1934 and their correspondence seems to have ended in the thirties. But the

friendship somehow remained. Once while Pound was at
Saint Elizabeth's, Dorothy Pound wrote Hemingway that
it was not true, as reported in European newspapers, that
Ezra had attacked him. Hem's reply was touching—
Hemingway at his best as a man: "I read every day that
people have attacked me, and I do not believe it, any more
than I believe we did not live on rue Notre-Dame-des-
Champs in the good old days." After Pound was released
from Saint Elizabeth's, Hemingway sent him a check for
$1500. Pound could well have used the money. Instead he
had the check framed in plastic as a souvenir. "Hem had a
genius for friendship," Pound told a reporter after that
novelist had passed away.

When Hemingway was awarded the Nobel Prize for
Literature in 1954 he said simply that he would have been
happy if Pound had received it instead, and suggested that
Pound be released from Saint Elizabeth's. "This is a good
year for releasing poets," he declared. Zenobia Jiménez,
wife of Juan Ramón Jiménez, who won the same prize
two years later, told me that this generous statement had
redeemed Hemingway in her husband's eyes; he had been
vexed because he believed Hemingway had misrepresented
Spanish life in *For Whom the Bell Tolls*.

While Jiménez was Professor of Spanish Literature at
Maryland University he visited Pound at Saint Elizabeth's
several times—a gentleman near sixty with a trim black
beard and burning eyes, dignified and noble in manner.
Mrs. Pound told me some years later: "He was something
very fine. I think I had not seen anything quite so *fine* before." At Saint Elizabeth's Pound and Jiménez conversed
in Spanish. "You are an exile *from* your country; I am an
exile *in* my country," Pound told him.

3

An Exile in His Own Land

Man is a gregarious animal, said Aristotle. In the gloomy halls of Saint Elizabeth's, Pound seized eagerly on personal contact with the outside world. Unfortunately, some of his most persistent visitors were themselves barely sane. Indeed, Pound felt that he was imprisoned in one lunatic asylum inside another; he often spoke of American society as a vast madhouse.

During Pound's twelve years of confinement at Saint Elizabeth's, his wife Dorothy visited him nearly every day. In all this time, she did not leave Washington, save for brief trips into the surrounding countryside. Occasionally she dined in downtown Washington with friends, preferring Chinese and Greek restaurants. She was not much in society. Pound had married his wife in 1914. Four decades later, she was gray, thoughtful, reserved, and serene, with a manner gracious and harmonious. Mrs. Pound seemed to live only for her husband; she read the books he read and, to all appearances, her thoughts were his. Pound's confinement obliged this lady of breeding to live in a drab and vulgar area near the hospital. She occupied rooms on 10th Place, S.E., and Brothers Place, S.E.—even the street names give the dreary atmosphere.

I remember Brothers Place: a jungle of wooden row houses fronted by porches with fake-Greek fluted columns, as if to mock the wife of a great Hellenist. Each house in the block was the same, but a few were losing more paint than others. And somewhere down the endless row lived Mrs. Pound, in a basement. You descended four or five steps; the screen door creaked. Mrs. Pound had just one room, which contained only books, a bed, and a writing desk. She smiled (maybe a bit grimly), and did not complain. One had the impression that externals mattered little to her; what counted was the time she had with her husband.

Though a flood of visitors appeared at Saint Elizabeth's over the years, some days none came except his wife. On Pound's sixty-ninth birthday I was there with Mrs. Pound and just one other. I presented him with a set of five Japanese teacups—thick, sturdy ones, black with undertones of red and brown. He turned them around in his hand, smiling profoundly, and said only "Yes, yes." When Pound showed pleasure, he did it with all his being. There was no gushing.

Among the regular visitors, about half were Social Crediters and half were literary people and professors. Curiously, only one of Pound's steady visitors kept coming regularly till the end of his Elizabethan Age: David Horton, a black-bearded giant, who served Pound as a kind of errand boy. Some would stop visiting after Pound quarreled with them and made them unwelcome; others, like myself, left Washington and afterward came to Saint Elizabeth's only occasionally. E. E. Cummings said to a friend, with precision: "In everyone's relations with Mr. Pound there come . . . coolnesses."

Pound's Jewish obsession was never absurder than in the way he sometimes rejected visitors. Though many Jews came to call on him and were received with the same courtesy as others, Pound had the strange custom of referring to an unliked visitor as Jewish—no matter if he had not a drop of Semitic blood, back to his remote ancestors. The poet Charles Olson, Swede in name and appearance, declared that he and Pound parted after Pound asked him about Jewish forebears. Olson (as he tells the story) then began recounting his genealogy, beginning with the earliest Olsons, and as he approached modern times shifted gradually into an ever-thickening Jewish accent. This was his last visit to Saint Elizabeth's.

Olson is considered the daddy of beatnik poetry, through his influence on Ginsberg, Kerouac, and others. If he is, Pound must be the grandfather, because Olson's verse mimics *The Cantos* even down to the typographical mannerisms, and the name "cantos" is even borrowed for some of it. He was one of Pound's first visitors in Washington, while Pound was still in the District Jail awaiting trial. Olson settled in Washington and visited the master frequently during the late nineteen-forties. By the time I appeared, Olson had dropped from the Saint Elizabeth's scene.

About Olson Pound would only say irritatedly that he was concerned with abstractions, not with verse (probably referring to Olson's theoretical essays about poetry). But perhaps the real reason Pound quarreled with Olson—and every other disciple except one—is expressed in what Yeats wrote of his own imitators:

Was ever dog that praised his fleas?

Most of the better known American poets visited Saint Elizabeth's: Eliot, Cummings, Williams, Marianne Moore, Allen Tate, Conrad Aiken, Elizabeth Bishop, Robert Lowell, Langston Hughes, and many others. H. L. Mencken came down from Baltimore before his last illness; he was one of the first visitors to Saint Elizabeth's. And Archibald MacLeish finally called on Pound in 1956.

MacLeish had been very much influenced by Pound's verse, and had drawn on its tricks for his own. He wrote of "the extraordinary vitality of Pound's work," and said, "Most work ages with time. His doesn't. It keeps the hard sharp glitter—the cutting edge." However, MacLeish's admiration for Pound's poetry was not reciprocated. Pound told me at Saint Elizabeth's that if the East had taught MacLeish only the exoticism of his poem "You, Andrew Marvell," he had not learned much. Politically the two poets had been on opposite sides—Pound bitterly against Franklin Roosevelt, MacLeish devoutly for. MacLeish had served as Assistant Secretary of State under Roosevelt; Pound had fiercely attacked both Roosevelt and MacLeish in his Rome Radio broadcasts. So for the first decade of Pound's incarceration, MacLeish did not visit him. In the early fifties, a Harvard colleague of MacLeish's told me that MacLeish had a bad conscience about this.

But at last he went for one visit. The two poets seem to have gotten along well (Mrs. Pound told me that MacLeish was *simpatico*), and MacLeish later wrote eloquently of his horror at witnessing "a conscious mind capable of the most complete awareness . . . incarcerated among minds which are not conscious and cannot be aware" and commented on "the patience and kindliness of the man who suffers it."

Of the regular literary visitors, I liked best a tiny, withered lady, nearly deaf, in her late eighties: Edith Hamilton. She and her lady companion came to Saint Elizabeth's once a week, for a time, in a long black car driven by a liveried chauffeur. Later she said she was too tired for regular visits. She and Pound were a pleasant contrast: she small, demure, and slyly humorous, Pound broad-shouldered and vigorous, with a Latin vivacity.

Miss Hamilton had traveled and studied to please herself

and served as principal of a Baltimore girls' school until she was fifty, then began to write. "My writing method is simple," she told me. "I put down exactly what I think." This combination of forthrightness and knowledge was perhaps what made her books about Greek and Roman civilization so effective and popular. She was too wise in her subject to be a pedant.

I had tea with Miss Hamilton and her companion in the neat walled garden of her Massachusetts Avenue home, near Georgetown in Washington. Birds sang, and I discussed that turbulent old poet with this delicate aged lady. "Alas, I do not understand *The Cantos*," she declared, "although I am fond of some of his earlier poetry." I replied: "We in America do not honor our poets. Therefore the poet throws his work in the public's face, not caring if it does or does not understand." "Ah, you have opened the door a bit," she said generously.

We spoke of Mr. Pound's recent work, and she told me: "His translations of Confucius . . . compared with the Greek philosophers, I do feel . . . oh, but you must not tell him. . . . I would *never* say it to him. . . ." I assured her that I was discretion personified. "They are just . . . just a bit"—her sparrow eyes regarded me—"*platitudinous!*"

As if to soften this severity, she then expressed doubt as to whether translation of *any* artwork were possible. And she said: "Mr. Pound knows more Greek and Latin literature than I, although it is my specialty, and besides that he knows far more French and German." Some years afterward, I sent her a Christmas present from Japan—a booklet with photographs of Japanese handicrafts, which had cost about twenty-five cents. "This was the nicest present I received for Christmas this year," she wrote me. When Miss Hamilton passed away, a graciousness left the world.

Pound's early Saint Elizabeth's years had been enlivened

by a first-rate scandal: *l'affaire Bollingen.* He had had the
temerity to compose the best poetry published in the
United States during 1948, *The Pisan Cantos.* This obvious
fact was recognized by a committee of fourteen leading
American authors, and Pound was therefore awarded the
first $1,000 Bollingen Prize for Poetry by the Library of
Congress. In recommending Pound for this prize, the ad-
visory committee's Fellows stated: "The Fellows are aware
that objections may be made to awarding a prize to a man
situated as is Mr. Pound. . . . [But] to permit other considerations than that of poetry achievement to sway the decision would destroy the significance of the award and
would in principle deny the validity of that objective perception of value on which civilized society must rest."

The last words—*that objective perception of value on
which civilized society must rest*—are a classic definition.

However, the howls of protest shook, if not Olympus, at
least the offices of *Poetry* magazine. *The Saturday Review
of Literature* published violent attacks on the award and
Pound, congressmen were up in arms, and the poor Library
of Congress had to divest itself of Bollingen Prize-awarding
functions, which were taken over by Yale University.
Even Radio Moscow got into the act, commenting: "One is
prompted to ask how low and miserable must be the quality of modern bourgeois poetry in America if even the insane and verified ravings of a confessed madman could win
a literary prize?"

Pound, at Saint Elizabeth's, pretended a vast indifference
to the whole matter, and referred to the prize as the
"Bubble-Gum Prize." Then *Poetry* magazine, under Hayden Carruth's editorship, published a pamphlet defending
Pound against *The Saturday Review*'s fury—with state-
ments by a number of important poets—whereupon the
trustees of *Poetry* honored the great American tradition of

free speech and expressed their gratitude to the man who had once done more than anyone to establish *Poetry* as a distinguished magazine, by firing Hayden Carruth. As usual, E. E. Cummings had the last word to say about the matter:

> Re Ezra Pound—poetry happens to be an art;and artists happen to be human beings.
>
> An artist doesn't live in some geographical abstraction,superimposed on a part of this beautiful earth by the nonimagination of unanimals and dedicated to the proposition that massacre is a social virtue because murder is an individual vice. Nor does an artist live in some soi-disant world,nor does he live in some socalled universe, nor does he live in any number of "worlds" or in any number of "universes." As for a few trifling delusions like the "past" and "present" and "future" of quote mankind unquote,they may be big enough for a billion super mechanized submorons but they're much too small for one human being.
>
> Every artist's strictly illimitable country is himself.
>
> An artist who plays that country false has committed suicide;and even a good lawyer cannot kill the dead. But a human being who's true to himself—whoever himself may be—is immortal;and all the atomic bombs of all the anti-artists in spacetime will never civilize immortality.

Cummings and his wife also came to Saint Elizabeth's now and then. In his Greenwich Village apartment, Cummings told me he was watching a bluejay on the Saint Elizabeth's lawn when it struck him that this belligerent and beautiful bird was Pound's totem. (Cummings believed in totems; his own, he thought, was the elephant.) A Cummings poem in praise of a bluejay, written about this time, seems to derive from that moment of recognition. Pound is also the unnamed subject of an earlier Cummings poem ("this mind made war / being generous . . .") in which Pound is called "almost this god."

"Pound is for the poetry of this century what Einstein is for its physics," Cummings wrote. For his part, Cummings may have taught Pound to care for the typographical arrangement of words on the page; in this respect, compare the later Cantos, written after Pound had read Cummings, with the earlier. Personally the two poets had long had a warm affection for each other, though Cummings maintained humorously that Pound's economic preoccupations frightened him. Rolf Fjelde described to me Cummings undoing the wrapper of a book Pound had sent him, with mock shudders lest the subject be economics.

William Carlos Williams was another occasional Saint Elizabeth's visitor. In his autobiography, Williams took a just measure of Pound's mind as he observed it at Saint Elizabeth's:

> I can't understand how Pound has been so apparently unmoved by his incarceration, guilty or essentially innocent as he may be. His mind has not budged a hair's breadth from his basic position, he has even entrenched himself more securely in it—recently finding precedents in the writings of a certain Controller of the Currency sixty or seventy-five years ago, who held similar views on our official perfidies. Pound has privileges, it must be acknowledged, and is kindly treated by the hospital personnel. But he does not waste them. He works constantly, reads interminably. The curator of the Oriental Library in Washington brings him the texts he is interested in when he wants them; he has the Greek of whoever it may be to decipher and understand. He may translate; he has his typewriter; his erudition is become more and more fearsome as time passes, whatever the outcome is to be.

Pound sent many of his callers on to Williams, who seemed to be an especially dear old friend, prized even more because their areas of disagreement were stimulating. But I remember him once grumping about Williams' readiness to talk with people too dull to bother about, in Pound's view: "Bill Williams would converse with a goat if he were amiable."

Pound was a man of all the arts. His book *Gaudier-Brzeska* is an eloquent appreciation of that sculptor sacrificed to World War I. He wrote articles praising the sculptor Jacob Epstein and the maker of ancient instruments Arnold Dolmetsch (in the Paris years, he had tried his hand at sculpting himself). From 1917 to 1920 he was music critic for *The New Age*. He was a pianist, more enthusiastic than skillful. He even composed two operas, *The Testament* and *Cavalcanti*, and his book *Antheil, and the Theory of Harmony* is a venture into music criticism. During the Rapallo days, he had worked on music scores, filling in the bass parts of Vivaldi works that the composer had not transcribed.

At Saint Elizabeth's, younger workers in all the arts—writers, painters, sculptors, and composers—came to visit Pound. His extraordinary helpfulness to young people, so renowned during forty or fifty years, was still very much in evidence. He had a teacher's instincts, and was constantly trying to explain and guide. But, as a good teacher, Pound was not domineering; he received contrary opinions in good grace, and they seemed to amuse him. In fact, he had more tolerance than many professional tolerators. I never knew a man with such passionately held opinions who was so open to disagreement.

"We agreed to disagree," Pound said of his relations to T. S. Eliot, perhaps his greatest disciple. He wrote Douglas McPherson in 1939: "When I go onto a tennis court I don't want the young to send me a soft service even if I am the oldest living purrformer except Gustav of Sweden. Why shd. a writer want it soft from young critics? Naturally, a hard service gets a hard return. One wants a hard ball *in* the court; i.e., pertinent to matter in hand." In *The Cantos,* Pound retells a story of Confucius: The master asks each of his disciples to say how they would act if they were lord of a province. They do so, then one inquires which had answered correctly. Said Confucius, "They have all answered correctly, that is to say, each in his own nature." This was basically Pound's attitude.

The title of Pound's earlier verse collection, *Personae* (roles, masks), gives a key to his own character. He had an unusual ability to get outside his self and understand others' personalities. This helps explain his skill as a translator. In *The Cantos* the masks are sometimes changed with such bewildering rapidity that we feel the work becomes "a broken bundle of mirrors"—Pound's phrase in "Near Perigord." In his personal dealings too he had this ability to objectify himself. Yet, curiously, in more abstract areas, such as politics, he found it hard to see objectively.

Pound always talked with young people as if they were age equals. And, conversely, when he was young (Mrs. Pound recalled) he had the ability of conversing with much older people as if there were no age difference. There was indeed a certain timelessness about him. Though he was forty-three years older than me, I never felt it. I think Pound even preferred talking with the young, for they at least had the hope of improvement. In Canto 13 he cites Confucius

> "Respect a child's faculties
> "From the moment it inhales the clear air,
> "But a man of fifty who knows nothing
>   Is worthy of no respect."

At Saint Elizabeth's the master would often flatter young people by indicating to them that he prized them more than the big shots of the literary world—and he did.

Pound tried to help anyone who came to him for help at Saint Elizabeth's. Guy Davenport told me how once when he visited there he found a red-haired actress weeping and pouring out her troubles while Pound patiently held her hands and consoled her. This lasted the entire visiting time, much to Davenport's disgust, because he had traveled to Washington especially to see Pound and hardly had a chance to speak with him. "Her father is a rabbi," Pound said later. This story may be set against the general impression that Pound was anti-Jewish; on a personal level, at least, he was usually not.

For forty years before his incarceration, Pound had been active as literary entrepreneur: bringing artists together, arranging for publication, propagandizing for new writers, editing, and so on. Beginning with his Rapallo days he had done less of this, for, having struggled with the taste of several generations, Pound felt that the later ones should be left to their own decisions. "After the age of fifty, one cannot be a telephone directory of young writers," he said at Saint Elizabeth's when asked which recent poets he preferred. While in the "bug-house" he wrote no literary criticism; his only literary labors were on *The Cantos* and translations from Chinese and Greek.

Nevertheless the old instincts remained. At Saint Elizabeth's Pound quietly but steadily tried to stir up ferment in the arts by bringing people together. Contact was essential, he believed. Many visitors left Saint Elizabeth's with a name scribbled on a scrap of paper by the master; and an introduction from Pound was good nearly anywhere. My own experience was typical. I went to Puerto Rico taking a note: "J. R. Jimenez. This is M. Reck. Ezra Pound." But, sad to say, that noble Spanish poet was by then victim of a madness worse than Pound's, and quite different—if Pound was indeed mad. He suffered from melancholia, and stayed at home with the shades drawn. So the note was never presented. I chatted with Jiménez' wife, sitting in the evening on the veranda of his home while the poet muttered and shouted to himself inside. Pound wrote May 14, 1955, in his usual ebullient manner: ". . . AND words of cheer to Juan Ram if they are any use." They weren't.

Mrs. Jiménez was dying in the hospital when the news arrived that her husband had won the 1956 Nobel Prize for Literature. He survived her by only a year and a half, and his depression never left him. At Saint Elizabeth's, Pound attributed Jiménez' mental state to the low caliber of the students at Maryland University, where he had been teaching. Mrs. Jiménez told me this was incorrect, and his experiences at the University had in fact been quite agreeable.

Pound's friendships extended even to Japan, and when I went there he was as usual ready with introductions—first to Michio Ito, a friend from London days. Ito told me he had left Japan as a teen-age boy and gone to France where, being an exotic, he was a sensation in cultivated drawing rooms. "What is art?" he would ask everywhere. In Paris he met Debussy and Rodin. About 1914 he moved to London, presumably still trying to find out what art is. Ito had known no classical Japanese drama when he left his homeland, but in London he found that it was the rage, because Pound's versions of the Noh had just appeared. So he studied Noh not in Japan but in London, and when Yeats began writing plays in Noh style, Ito danced the role of the Guardian of the Well in the first performance of *At the Hawk's Well* (1916). Canto 78 reports Ito's summary of Japanese choreography

> "Jap'nese dance all time overcoat" he remarked
> with perfect precision

Therefore I expected to meet an Ito speaking pidgin English. On the contrary, he proved to be a stocky white-haired gentleman who had several mansions in Tokyo, was engaged in promoting various cultural activities such as girlie shows and model schools, for which he was very famous in Japan, and had spent the years between the two world wars—in Hollywood! He spoke an excellent American English.

But this Japanese Sam Goldwyn was by no means a fool. He told me about a superb Spanish dancing team he had once seen, fiery and graceful—perfection! Then he had gone backstage to talk with them. "And, you know," said Ito, "they had absolutely nothing to say!" In other words, art is doing, not talking about it.

And in his quiet, measured voice, amid the stillness of his Tokyo home, Ito spoke about his friend of four decades before:

"If I saw Ezra today, I would give him a massage and say: . . . relax."

A shower of Pound letters brought me to Kitasono Katue, leader of Japanese avant-garde poetry and Pound's correspondent since the nineteen-thirties. "He's a dentist," Pound had told me. It turned out that he was librarian of a dental college—and looked the part: shy and wearing especially thick glasses. He met every Sunday afternoon with his coterie; I attended several times and tried to understand. Kitasono had a biting wit. When he did not like a poem, he would say, "No smoke rises from that chimney."

Pound had written of Kitasono's group, the Vou Club: "All the moss and fuzz that for 20 years we have been trying to scrape off our language, these young men start without it. They see the crystal set, the chemical laboratory and the pine tree with untrammeled clearness. . . . Nowhere in Europe is there any such vortex of poetic alertness. Tokio takes over where Paris stopped." Kitasono gave me a typed history of this leading Japanese poetic group which had become one of the fragments Pound had "shored against his ruin":

The Vou Club

by Kitasono Katue

The Vou Club was born in 1935. The members at the start were Kitasono Katue, Iwamoto Shuzo, Miki Tei, and eleven other poets. The initial number of the magazine *Vou* was issued on the 5th of July in the same year, containing four essays on poetry, fifteen poems and the translation of a letter of Jack Vasse.

I can remember the moment in which the strange name Vou was adopted by us. It was on the table of a small coffeehouse on the Ginza street. We had been satisfied with none of the names introduced there, each of them having its own meaning restrictive to our activities, when we hit upon the meaningless spell which Iwamoto was scribbling automatically on a scrap of paper, and thus we became Vouists.

The Vou poets wanted to create a new trend of art in Tokio entirely different from those which were already born after the First World War. To begin with, we needed to break up every traditional and conventional art in Japan. We decided that we should be as ironical in our artistical attitude as Eric Saty [*sic*] who fought for modern music.

In *Vou*'s third issue we printed Abstraction-Creation Art Non Figurative, and Boethy's essay in the fourth issue. I specially mention this, because I wish to suggest the direction of art of the Vou group at this time.

In the beginning of 1936 the members of our group counted 21, several composers, painters, and technologists having joined us. In May of the year we held the Vou Club demonstration at the hall of the Denki Club,

[A portrait of Ezra Pound taken by Boris de Rachewiltz
at Schloss Brunnenberg during the autumn of 1958.]

RK/ re TRAX /
                dont bother about the WORDS , translate the meaning.
in the spoken parts/ dialog , this should be CLEAR , and be what
the speaker would SAY if getting over the meaning in japanese. NOW
        in the XOROI , go for the FEELING. The two KINDS of language
are quite different / in the first real people are speaking/
        saying what carries forward the action / in the XOROI they
are singing (except the few lines marked "spoken "/
        Ito cd/ do some fine chorography for the Analolu / xorus.

The troops have come HOME/ whoops. there is no need for more than
one voice , most of the time/ *then repeat contrapunto , one voice*
                        a lot of voices might blur the words. *a*
The greek will do you no good , unless the jap chorus could   *Time*
get closer to the greek rhythm , than fHHHH in working from the   *hover*
english/ BUT it is not the least necessary to copy either/   *No le*
        it is a case of getting the equivalent feeling.   *+ to*
The form of the play is magnif/ everythim fits / Daysair goes   *as ec*
INTO the tragic mask. Herak emerges from it .   *as*
        TRAX in anithesis to Antig/ and other Soph/ plays in   *neg*
that NO ONE has any evil intentions, NO bad feeling , vendetta   *ext*
or whatso . All of 'em trying to be nice/ BUT the tragedy moves
on just the same.
        Daysair , Queen and woman/ top of all greek descriptive
writing in the Nurse's description of her before the suicide. HERAK/
tough guy who is also a God.

        Dont bother with words or linguistic constructions /
the people are alive / the speech is clear and natural.

        (Various people fussing about colloquialism. What one wants
is what a Jap Daysair, or Hyllos or messenger would SAY. under
the circs/ NOT a copy of english grammar/
        In the sung parts , be as classic as you like / drag in
phrases from Noh itself if they fit and intensify the situation.
(I dont recall any in particular, but there might be some or
some that wd/ recall great Noh lines.).   *st. to hr.*
                                                          gone well
reading in N.Y. with cello and kettle drum acc/ the Xoroi.
B.B.C. transmitting it on or about Apr/ 25. I dont spose Tokyo
gets London 3rd/ program.
        Ito to do anything he likes. ko GUN   fun-TOooo .
(He will be sorry to hear that Dulac is dead , if he hasn't heard it
already.)
    D.P. sending two Hud/ in case F.M. dont step on the gas
at once. You can ask me re/ partic/ passages , naturally.
The Venus is practically naked behind that gauze curtain/ I
dont know quite how naked a jap goddess can be in apparition/ at any
rate from the coptch up . She aint eggzakly a Kuanon / but
the willow bough cd/ be brought in definitely. she cd/ hold one.
Goacher who is doing the Hyllos for BBC/ has sent on some prize best-
ialities in other translations. They dont even understand that LAMPRA.
        after that phrase Herak who has been cursing D/ for a
bitch   never utters a reproach. THAT is like the transformation
in Noh.
        Do they, or do you know that the last message I got thru into
U.S. press was: we shd/ GIVE Guam to the Japs, but INsist on having
300 sound films of Noh in exchange.   (And how damn much better
THAT wd/ have been .) Don't lie down on the fight to get sound films
of actual Noh. some bloody foundation / bastids pouring out

millions for scholastic fugg.
                                                        over

2/ even " grammar ╪ dont matter if the speech is alive/ it can
be ungrammatical IF it is the way people speak / the way a
Queen , or a hobo , speaks NOW in Japan. Day/ is an aristo/

and also sensitive , very delicately. The Hyllos the next role
in so ╪ far i╪/ HHH as it requires understanding presentation.
That is why I am so glad to have got Goacher for it. They say their
BBC Herak/ is a colossus wHHH who can roar. The nurse narrates
so that is less difficult /

                         but Ito might do a choric dance
, combine a choric movement to occur . silently while she is
describing the suicide. IN fact , all the intelligence they have
got can be turned on / and let 'em ENjoy themselves.

Benton, next in Sq $/ series.

    One misprint in Hud/ PUT there in print shoppe AFTER
    proofs were corrected / i.e. Nemean NOT Newman
         herdsman.   read)

    ALZO/ p. 511 , enter Nurse.
                    Better she also enter in a tragic
        mask (small mask, quite different from Daysair's)
        The Minoru will understand difference.

                                         after. saluti
                                            D. P.

[This letter (March 12, 1954) sends instructions for translating Sophocles and
fitting it into the Japanese Noh drama form. Pound had made an English version of Sophocles' *Women of Trachis*, with the dedication:

A version for Kitasono Katue, hoping he will use it on my dear old
friend Miscio Ito, or take it to the Minoru if they can be persuaded to
add to their repertoire.

The Minoru are an ancient family of Noh actors. Fujitomi Yasuo and I tried a
Japanese translation, which would, we hoped, be metamorphosed into a Noh
play by a Noh expert. The Army shipped me back to the States before our
translation was completed.

RK   = Reck
TRAX = *Women of Trachis*
xoroi   = choruses, xoros = chorus
Herak = Herakles
Dulac = the painter Edmund Dulac, a common London acquaintance of
          Pound and Ito in the nineteen-tens
Hud/   = *The Hudson Review*, who first published Pound's *Women of
          Trachis*
F.M.   = Frederick Morgan, editor of same
Benton = William Hart Benton, nineteenth-century Missouri senator admired
          by Pound
Sq $ = the "Square Dollar" series of pamphlets, issued by David Horton
          under Pound's aegis
Sette = literary magazine edited by Fujitomi Yasuo
saludos
a todos = greetings to all (Spanish)
D.P.   = Dorothy Pound]

Based on D.P.'ʿ report that there is hope.   As I have always loathed
reading, and can now read practically nothing save to learn what
I don't know / FACTS .

Suggest ᴴeck consider following points, as to whether he wants
to revise   before F.P. attempts.

NOT necessary to translate adjectives (epithets) by adjectives.

Note Selloi , in TRAX / chaps sleep there on the ground.
                or something like that.

        rather than the on_thegroundsleeping .

In short. ᴴeck   reread   3 books to see if ANYWHERE still bitched

            by the SYNTAX of the original. The sense of the original

shd/ be retained, NOTthe syntax.

Salels   rusé personnage / that HITS. sometimes there IS
            an adjective, but the personnage ..
                                    gives the life to
            that trans/

Has ᴴeck at ANY point taken his eye off the THING , in trying
            to follow the original LANGUAGE ?

            he/
I take it/has a carbon/ praps he might like to revise and then
 swap for uncorrected copy now in WashDC.

I dont know from D/ what ᴴeck's " metre" is.
Prosody : the articulation of the total sound of a poem , whether
            of 2 lines or 200 cantos.

Nobody will care a damn about the regularity of the metre.

    Does ᴴeck think Homer's metre is very IRREGULAR ?
            has he considered that possibility or fact ??

nobody will care a damn about the metre if there is FLOW.

[I had begun a verse translation of *The Iliad*. This letter (May 17, 1955) contains tips for translating Homer.

D.P. and D/ = Dorothy Pound
TRAX   = Sophocles' *Women of Trachis*, which Pound had recently
            translated
Salel   = Hugues Salel, sixteenth-century French translator of Homer.
            "Rusé personnage" is Salel's rendition of Odysseus' epithet
            polymetis.]

in which we read eight manifestos and recited poems of our own. This attempt was rather a failure as there came up only a few opponents.

I had sent copies of *Vou* to Ezra Pound, who soon sent to me from Rapallo a copy of *Guido Cavalcanti* and a letter with his affectionate hail that the Vou group would remain forever in the youth of twenty-one. He gave us as many opportunities of touching the avant-garde of England and America as he could. If *Vou* still keeps the youth of twenty-one (as I am sure of it), it's much indebted to his sensible suggestions.

In 1937 through Ezra Pound I knew D. C. Fox, member of Forschungsinstitut für Kulturmorphologie supervised by Leo Frobenius, and I published the very interesting essay Paideuma in *Vou*'s sixteenth issue. It was in this same issue that the Vou poet Fuji Takeshi treated of T. E. Hulme's *Speculations* in his article "The Direction of Poetry as a View of the World."

In February 1937 I sent to Pound sixteen Vou poems with my notes, which were printed the next year in the first number of *The Townsman* started by Ronald Duncan, with Pound's introductory notes for them. This was the first appearance of Vou poems to Europe, and the next year James Laughlin in America printed fourteen Vou poems with his notes in New Directions. The war between China and Japan already began in July 1937. We hoped it would soon be finished, but on the contrary it was marching to the death fight of the Pacific War. The government began to stiffen even on art. Some of the surrealists were imprisoned. In 1940 we were forced at last to abandon publication of the magazine. I succeeded somehow or other in keeping Vou poets from arrest.

On December 8th 1941, I heard, in the library of the Nippon Dental College (the librarian of which I have been from then till now), the radio news of the attack on Pearl Harbor. Fortunately there came an interval in which the pressure on culture was a little slacked, and I could reissue the magazine under the title *New Technics*, with the contents just the same as before. It lasted four numbers and then ceased as the army persecuted again every movement of international tendencies. We diverted ourselves in cultivating the classical field of Japanese literature. I began printing the literary pamphlet *Mugi* (wheat), which was continued until the beginning of 1945 when Tokio was exhaustively bombed out.

In August Japan surrendered. I caught on the radio the Emperor's voice in the Ichijoin Temple in Sanjo, a small town three hundred kilometers from Tokio. Vou poets came back from the war by twos and threes, and in 1947 we revived the magazine *Vou*. After numbers 31 and 32, the inflation in this country forced us to give up the next issue.

It was by the backing of Asagi press that we could begin publication of the newly titled *Cendre*, which was put out six times until 1949 when Asagi got into depression. In January of this year we again put the title back to *Vou* and published the thirty-third and thirty-fourth issues aided by the Shoshinsha press.

Vou's orientation: everything humanistic is a boredom. Tears, cryings, loves, crimes, ironies and humors, all attract us in no ways. We only find a little of aesthetic excitement in erasing every humanistic vestige from art.

"Everything tends to be angular"—T. E. Hulme.

I found *Vou* lively, but its "anti-humanistic" doctrine a hard one—understandable, perhaps, as an antidote to lachrymose poetizing, but after all one *is* a human being oneself. From a friend I learned something curious: Kitasono could not understand much of Pound's letters to him. No wonder, since even an English-language poet can have difficulties with them (the references in Pound's letters are as little identified as in *The Cantos*). Yet it shows strikingly that inability to find a way of communicating with his audience which plagued Pound.

Also Pound brought me to Fujitomi Yasuo, a younger avant-garde poet whose verse has a delightful humor. Fujitomi was producing an international poetry magazine called *Sette*—in English and Italian—*on the typewriter!* He typed out twenty or thirty copies himself on vari-colored paper; one went to Pound, who sent him my address. As a result of our talks, Fujitomi began translating E. E. Cummings—for the first time into Japanese, save for one version of the early *Tulips and Chimneys*. He subse-quently published several books of Cummings translations (the last reached Cummings the day before his death) and founded a magazine entitled *i*, devoted entirely to Cum-mings. So as far away as Japan Pound's germinating influ-ence was felt during the nineteen fifties.

Confucius had said that he could learn something from anybody; Pound too had the amiable quality of being an excellent listener. In the mid-fifties Quincy Howe, Jr., and another Harvard undergraduate started a very lively lit-erary magazine and naturally thought of asking Pound to contribute. So they traveled to Saint Elizabeth's. Pound told them he had nothing (in fact, he made no contribu-tions to literary magazines while in the "bug-house") but he would like to hear what *they* had to say. Whereupon they conversed with him for two hours. Pound was ready to learn from persons almost fifty years his junior.

In addition to such casual callers, Pound attracted a num-ber of disciples to Saint Elizabeth's. He had written in *Per-sonae* about "the pleasing attitudes of discipleship," and ap-parently his Washington followers pleased him, at least for a time. But his more perceptive visitors saw they were an unhealthy lot, and at least one old friend, Olga Rudge, urged him to chase them all out. And eventually Pound *did* evict all except David Horton. While his patience lasted, they entertained him, and he used them to run errands for him. Confucius had written: "I want madcaps for my disciples." Pound had them.

The most flamboyant was Dallam Simpson, a flaming redhead who aped Pound's thoughts, gestures, speaking manner, and beard. About 1950 Pound, perpetually generous, had given him an authorization to draw on royalties that could not be removed from various European countries, and he made a trip to Europe. In Paris he went about with Pound's son Omar. When Pound's old friends saw them they said, *"Ah, vous êtes le fils de Monsieur Pound"* —to him, not to Omar, he looked so much like the young Ezra Pound.

At Pound's instigation, Simpson compiled and published the first collection of verse by Basil Bunting, a Pound follower from prewar times and a vigorous craftsman who should be better known than he is. But Simpson prefaced the collection with a ludicrously pretentious essay, which prevented it from being published in England by a first-rate house, Faber and Faber. T. S. Eliot, the Faber editor, refused to take the book on unless the preface were removed; and Bunting, a stubborn English Quaker, thought that since Simpson had done the collecting and editing job, the preface should stay. The deadlock was never resolved. Simpson quarreled with Pound in the early nineteen-fifties, and disappeared in the direction of Mallorca.

For the disciples, Pound was not a poet but a Cause. Eustace Mullins was a small-town Virginian who became an ardent convert to Pound's economic ideas. He seemed to have no spine, and floated rather than walked. After Pound's release, he produced a rambling "biography," *This Difficult Individual, Ezra Pound* (Fleet Publishing Corporation, 1961). The book's blurb vaunts the fact that the master called the author "the Mulligator." Pound had found the right word, for Mullins was distinctly saurian. Yet the fact is that over a decade—at least off and on— Pound trusted Mullins, confided in him, and used him to run errands.

In his "biography," Mullins writes patronizingly about nearly everybody—including Hemingway, Eliot, Yeats— except himself and Pound. "As a Virginian I knew defeat; therefore I was able to know culture," Mullins declares, and the book is full of similar murky pretentiousness. Pound, in Italy when it appeared, was not pleased with it, and refused to talk of it.

Among the wild visitors that Mullins brought the master was a former newspaperman named Rex Lampman, who dressed strangely and had an unrestrained imagination. Mullins enjoyed smuggling Lampman, with his eccentric clothes, into elegant gatherings of society literati in Washington, where his presence was not at all appreciated. But Lampman and Pound got along handsomely, and the 1958 edition of Pound's critical book *Pavannes and Divagations* begins with an epitaph for the author

> Here he lies, the Idaho kid,
> the only time he ever did.
>
> Rex Lampman

Another of Pound's younglings, John Kasper, swam in from New York City sometime in the early fifties. Kasper achieved notoriety in 1957 when he drifted south to make rabble-rousing speeches against racial integration and got himself jailed in several places. At that time Pound's release from Saint Elizabeth's was brewing, and Kasper's adventures very likely delayed the release for a year, for Pound and Kasper were mentioned together in newspaper reports, and there was some feeling that Pound was responsible for what Kasper did. Whether he was or not, the Lord only knows. On some occasions Pound might have wanted to say—as Karl Marx reputedly did about the Marxists—"I am not a Poundian."

Kasper certainly aped Pound's ideas; and in American politics, the master always took the conservative (hence the "states' rights") side. But one friend who visited Saint Elizabeth's while Kasper was there told me he heard Pound sharply rebuking Kasper for his activities in the South. Pound himself was, if anything, prejudiced *in favor of* Negroes. "I like a number of shades in my landscape," he wrote in *The Pisan Cantos*. The Negro GIs Pound saw at Pisa are described with admiration and affection.

> thank Benin for this table ex packing box
> "doan yu tell no one I made it"
> > from a mask as fine as any in Frankfurt
> "It'll get you offn th' groun"

(Pound is referring to the African masks at the Frobenius Institute in Frankfurt.) And only someone who, like myself, was raised in Washington, D.C., can fully savor this passage from Canto 95

> Elder Lightfoot is not downhearted,
> Elder Lightfoot is cert'nly
> > not
> > > downhearted,
> He observes a design in the Process.

The Elder Lightfoot Michaux was a riproaring Negro preacher who exhorted his faithful in great meetings at Griffith Stadium—a very much alive man with a real poetic rhythm in his voice. Pound heard him on the radio at Saint Elizabeth's, and described him as he was: one who had an insight into the process of nature.

I had a singular introduction to another disciple, a part-Indian Mexican "artist type" who roomed with Horton in a dingy unfurnished flat in downtown Washington. One day I stopped by the flat, and the Mexican was present. His sole occupation while I was there was throwing a knife into the bare floor, drawing it out, throwing it in again and again. He never once looked up. My flesh crept.

Pound not only tried to nourish the minds of his young followers, he even fed some of them. A certain McNaughton appeared in the late Saint Elizabeth's years, wearing a pince-nez and looking very much like photographs of the youthful William Butler Yeats. He drove a taxi for a living, and harangued his customers about the ideas of the master. The taxi business was not very lucrative, so Pound would save food from the lunches served to the Saint Elizabeth's inmates and pass it on to him at visiting hours. I remember him once peeping into a package the great twentieth-century poet had handed him. Was it a text of Confucius? Homer? A new set of Cantos? No. "Mmmm, bacon, lettuce, and tomato," said that taxi driver.

If this account of Pound's discipledom sounds like a rogues' gallery, it might be added that many of the regular Saint Elizabeth's visitors were even more or less respectable. Several Catholic University professors came out often, including the very sober English literature scholar J. C. La Driere. Despite his intellectual bias against professors, Pound often got along surprisingly well with academic persons. Rudd Fleming, professor of English at Maryland University, appeared every week with his wife Polly through most of the Saint Elizabeth's years. He would bring a thermos jug of excellent Chinese tea, and he and Pound would discuss Greek things, which were his passion. But toward the end of Mr. Pound's Elizabethan Age there ensued the inevitable "coolness." Perhaps the root of it was

Fleming's obtuseness concerning the Ezraic economic theories, but Pound was heard muttering about "sterile Hellenism."

Achilles Fang of Harvard, a man with an intolerance of mediocrity equal only to Pound's, occasionally took the train down from Cambridge to visit Saint Elizabeth's. In addition to being probably the most learned of all classical Chinese scholars (at least in a strictly lexicographic sense), Fang had an enormous personal library of Greek and Latin classics. He compiled a huge collection of notes on *The Pisan Cantos*—at one point reportedly a thousand pages, with a thousand more planned!! Then he went on to studying and annotating *Finnegan's Wake*. Fang wrote the introduction to Pound's translation of the Confucian Odes, published by the Harvard University Press in 1954.

Professor Norman Holmes Pearson of the Yale English Department also appeared from time to time. He kept a note pad handy and would scribble down what Pound said on the spot. As far as I know, he was the only one of Pound's visitors to take notes. Let us hope he someday publishes them.

Rolf Fjelde, poet and an editor of the best American poetry magazine of its time, *The Yale Poetry Review*, provided Pound with humane talk when he came down from New York City. Pound did a great deal to find contributors for *The Yale Poetry Review* (later *Poetry New York*), and when Fjelde departed for an auto trip around the States, Pound made a list of "the most interesting people in America," whom he was to visit on the way.

Fjelde became one of Pound's circle after *The Yale Poetry Review* published a special Pound issue. He wrote me an amusing account of his first visit to Saint Elizabeth's: "I always suspected that the reason Pound took me up so eagerly in '48 was not *The Yale Poetry Review*, but the fact that my mother, feeling sorry for Mr. Pound's confined condition, went to the specialty food shop at Abraham & Straus and bought about two dozen gourmet items: black olives, cocktail oysters, cashews, etc. I presented the bagful on arrival, and EP and DP dug in, with little cries of delight as each item was brought to light."

Charles Olson was then lecturing Pound on his "projective verse" theories—which derived from Pound anyhow —and, perhaps to get Olson off his neck, Pound sent him on to Fjelde with the recommendation that he vent his ideas in *Poetry New York*. So Olson wrote his now renowned essay on "projective verse" for *Poetry New York*. Olson's thesis is that breath is the basic unit in verse, which may explain why his essay is so windy. Anyhow, it became very influential among young poets. William Carlos Williams picked it up and reprinted it in his autobiography, and it became a statement of poetics for the Black Mountain group (Robert Duncan, Robert Creeley, Cid Corman, Jonathan Williams, Denise Levertov, and so on), which someone recently called just about the only academy of American poetry in existence now. So, via Olson and Williams, Pound remains the main influence on American poetry.

The composer Frank Ledlie Moore had more self-confidence in Pound's presence than any other visitor I saw at Saint Elizabeth's. I think he even talked more than Pound when he was there, and the master seemed to enjoy his exuberance. Moore was a thin gregarious individual of about thirty who had moved from New York City to Washington to be near Pound and visit him regularly. He was one of the disciples Pound actually helped support by slipping him money from time to time. (Like almost all the disciples, he was poor as a churchmouse.) Pound interested him in studying Byzantine tonalities, in an attempt to get at the original music of the Greek drama, and Moore composed Greek-type music for the choruses of Pound's version of the Sophoclean *Women of Trachis*. Moore wrote me: "Pound and I talked about Greek drama and its music. We were both very excited about the possibility of creating not a Greek drama, but an American drama as valid for the people as the Greek. Pound said 'all drama is pussyfoot,' and yet we talked in terms of making it new, making it that great."

Moore sent me a delightful memoir of the day he first took the Greek-American sculptor Michael Lekakis to visit Pound: "We left him and he went back to his room. Just as we were walking away from the little door at the foot of the stairs (Dorothy, Mike, and me), we heard a shout and saw Pound, up in his window, leaning out and singing Greek verse to us at the top of his lungs. Happy, full of happiness, and playing the part of Homer."

I myself began visiting Pound in 1951 while I was a student at the Institute of Contemporary Arts there in Washington. Pound had read my poems and liked them, or at least saw some hope in them—and the news was reported to me by a disciple. That was my introduction to him. I had more languages than the other young members of the "tribe of Ez," which sometimes made me a prize pupil. But my relations with the master were not all smooth. Once he wrote me while I was in Japan—I do not remember why— "International friendships are made by mutual respect between honourable men, not by mutual pocket-picking." I replied stormily, getting a few things off my own chest. Surprisingly enough—or not surprising, if you knew Pound—his reply was amused and conciliatory. Pound could take it as well as dish it out.

A buoyant and whimsical visitor was Pound's son Omar —"Omar the Roamar" I called him because of his nomadic proclivities. He had been raised by his grandmother Olivia Shakespear in England. During World War Two he dodged buzz bombs in London, then by way of Basil Bunting (and by predestination of being named Omar?) took up Islamic studies. I suppose this was a way of getting out from under his father's shadow, Islam being one of the few cultural areas in which Ezra Pound had not staked out a claim. Like Ezra he had attended Hamilton College, and after studying Islamic matters at McGill University and teaching a while in Boston, he departed to be principal of the American School in Tangier. Omar wrote pleasantly trivial poetry, his best lines perhaps these, in mock rejoicing for the death of his friend Wyndham Lewis:

> Wyndham is dead, hurrah!
> the man who never praised a war.
> Death has rounded off his edges
> but it cannot kill the core.

I first saw Omar in Japan on his way back to America from a year's study in Persia. With a carpet under his arm (purchased on the last day in Teheran as an investment), he had ridden buses and hitchhiked across northern India, seen Singapore and Hong Kong, and ended in Tokyo almost broke. I suggested mounting the carpet and flying, but he haunted the wharves for weeks until the captain of a U.S.-bound American ship agreed to take him on the crew —though he was non-union and had never sailed.

Omar had a passion for privacy. When he boarded the ship, the captain flipped through his passport and asked "Any relation to Ezra Pound?" "May be," said Omar.

4

The Man Ezra Pound

"It is hard to imagine Ezra as ever having been a boy," Mrs. Pound said to me once. And the earliest account of Pound by a literary man—his University of Pennsylvania classmate William Carlos Williams—describes him as self-assured and conscious of a literary mission. He wrote in *Personae*

> You say that I take a good deal upon myself;
> That I strut in the robes of assumption

From his adolescent days, he did. Pound was one of the few —Whistler and Wagner were others—who play the part of genius and *are* it.

For all Pound's self-confidence, I found no arrogance in him. He was considerate, a good listener, and quite unpretentious. He did not fake. One of our literary witchdoctors described Pound in 1939 as a drawling aesthete who pretended to read Chinese poetry in the original and declared it "relaxing." This is so far from the Pound of twelve years later that I suspect deliberate misrepresentation. Louise Gebhard Cann wrote of him—and my impression was the same: "He was direct, open, American, and suggested by the sympathy of his look, 'I know how you feel about it.'"

I remember a visit to Saint Elizabeth's just after Hugh Kenner's *The Poetry of Ezra Pound* had appeared. When asked what he thought of the book, Pound would only say: "Git out yer shillelaghs, boys"—meaning that he hoped it would rouse discussion. Kenner had compared Pound to Samuel Johnson. "In any case," cooed one admirer, "Johnson did not know Chinese." "Neither do I," said Pound.

It was indeed difficult to imagine the magisterial Mr. Pound as a boy. Yet, paradoxically, there was much boyishness in him too; in his sixties, he had the gusto and heartiness of youth. Perhaps, rather than boyishness, this was simply a poet's directness. Poetry means seeing things anew and directly (and its intellectual elements are superadded). The poet revivifies, and thus keeps the language itself vital, for language grows by fresh perception, as when a primitive man sees the boat's ripples and calls them "sea spider web." Pound aimed at recreating the freshness of nature in his verse (*Make It New* is the powerful title of one of his critical works), and as a person he had a natural freshness too. This had made him feel at home among the spontaneous Italians. One Italian-American visitor at Saint Elizabeth's said of him: "A pure Mediterranean type."

Pound had a lusty love of telling jokes, and a good repertoire of them. When he told an Irish dialect story, he became for the moment an Irishman; when he told a Jewish story, he was a Jew. I remember Pound gustily reading aloud a story from the letter of an English friend, his voice rising and falling, and booming at the end. Two gentlemen meet on the street. The first: "What's *wrong?*" His friend: "SMITH found JONES in bed with his WIFE and SHOT 'EM BOTH DEAD." The first: "Mmm, could be worse." Friend: "*What* do you *MEAN*, could be worse?" "Well, 'TWAS *ME* WAS THERE THE NIGHT BEFORE!"

Then Pound throws his gray head back and his tangly beard shakes with laughter.

I thought that Pound's egoism stayed within decent bounds, at least insofar as it expressed itself toward other persons (rather than ideas). T. S. Eliot had described him in London four decades before:

> No one could have been kinder to younger men or to writers who, whether younger or not, seemed to him worthy and unrecognised. No poet, furthermore, was, without self-depreciation, more unassuming about his own achievement in poetry. The arrogance which some people have found in him, is really something else; and whatever it is, it has not expressed itself in an undue emphasis on the value of his own poems.

And at Saint Elizabeth's one felt he was the same. His "arrogance," if he had it, was an overconfidence concerning his mission in society, a tendency to think that he alone could save society. I remember once at Saint Elizabeth's, soon after *The Letters of Ezra Pound* were published, Pound said: "More interesting are the letters written *to* me. They would make a better collection."

Pound at Saint Elizabeth's, a man in his late sixties and early seventies, was incredibly swift-witted. One day, to help a friend translating the Spanish novel *La Celestina*, I was pondering how to give a rhymed English rendition of

> Mira Nero, de Tarpeya,
> a Roma cómo se ardía:
> gritos dan niños y viejos
> y él de nada se dolía.

I asked Pound if he could translate it in rhyme (vaguely wondering if he would notice a resemblance to Mussolini). With no hesitation whatsoever, he suggested:

Nero from Tarpeia
watched Rome a-burn.
Kids and old men cried out
but it didn't give him a turn.

"Could be done many other ways too," he said. (Mussolini went unmentioned.)

Pound's Elizabethan Age was a prolific period for him, in spite of all the hindrances of being in a madhouse with no privacy—or did the hindrances even stimulate him? About 1952 he again began working on *The Cantos*, which were now moving toward their Paradiso section. The hellhole of Saint Elizabeth's was a most unlikely place for writing a paradise. But Pound did. The Cantos written at Saint Elizabeth's present a paradise of a tenderness, delicacy, and clarity absent from literature since Dante—a paradise of the mind for Pound, a mighty achievement of will and concentration while he was surrounded by madmen every moment of the day. Cantos 85 to 95 appeared in 1956, Cantos 95 to 109 in 1958. At Saint Elizabeth's Pound also produced a translation of the Chinese Book of Songs, a miracle of re-creation, rendered Sophocles' *Women of Trachis* into a very lively English, and wrote fanatic political notes (anonymous) for David Horton's right-wing sheet, *Strike*. Despite his confinement, Pound was certainly not vegetating.

Pound talked little about his own poetry at Saint Elizabeth's. And I avoided asking for explanations, because the verse speaks for itself or not at all. Once I inquired why he had omitted the much-admired little poem "An Immorality" from later editions of *Personae*. "Just cut out the bric-a-brac," he said. Another time he spoke with irritation of a critic who had seen the decline of the West symbolized in "Beer bottle on the statue's pediment!" (Canto 7). "It's *only* a bottle, *not* a phallus," declared Pound.

It was hard to get Pound to read his own verse at Saint Elizabeth's; I asked him several times and he growled "not in voice." (Pretty women had the best luck in getting a reading.) One visitor who was there at Saint Elizabeth's when Pound recited *The Cantos* described his style as "like a Baptist preacher." Frank Moore heard him, and was very much impressed by the rhythm: "the beats like deep gongs, the chitchat parts read lightly."

Pound's manner was often rather truculent. Wyndham Lewis saw a lust for perfection as the heart of his character. Perhaps it was that passion which made him appear forbidding. T. S. Eliot wrote: "Pound [had] a passionate desire, not merely to write well himself, but to live in a period in which he could be surrounded by equally intelligent and creative minds. Hence his impatience." It would seem that all the sternness, the bitterness came from that lust for perfection. "Mr. Pound is humane, but not human," E. E. Cummings once said. Like the Old Testament Ezra, Pound preached his visions constantly.

His typical treatment of a new visitor to Saint Elizabeth's was to offer a lecture on Social Credit economics, unintentionally omitting just enough to leave the listener more in the dark than before. Yet he regarded Social Credit as the simplest thing in the world. Eustace Mullins reports in his biography of Pound that he heard the master declare fifty times "Keep some of the non-interest-bearing national debt in circulation as currency." (Mullins seems to regard this as an aspect of wisdom.) One friend of mine whom I brought to Saint Elizabeth's summarized Pound's harangue afterward: "He was saying that two plus two equals four." Pound appeared to care more about his opinions than about the person addressed. Like Lionel Johnson in Yeats' poem, he perhaps "loved his learning better than mankind."

However, the center of *The Cantos* is a rewording of

Descartes: *"Amo ergo sum"*—"I love, therefore am."
Pound does have the Confucian *jen*—benevolence, open-
heartedness—whose ideogram depicts a man standing beside two horizontal lines, his arms, which are opened to
take in. "What thou lovest well remains/ the rest is dross,"
he says in *The Pisan Cantos,* and all *The Cantos* can be seen
as a definition of what the poet loves. From this viewpoint,
the many expressions of hate and disgust in *The Cantos* appear as only the inverse of Pound's love.

At Saint Elizabeth's Pound's talk was often sharp. He
spoke scathingly of modern so-called civilization where
things are "made to sell and sell quickly" (Canto 45).
When asked "What do you think of contemporary American poetry?" he might say, with a mischievous smile,
"There is none." (Though other times he did praise Robert
Lowell.) After someone mentioned the most prominent
American literary critic, Pound declared, "All I know
about Edmund Wilson is that when he went to see Santayana he was surprised that Santayana had never heard of
him." A snide comment but, considering Wilson's slipshod
critique of Pound himself, written in the early nineteen-
twenties, perhaps not entirely unjustified. Wilson was writing journalism, and it had to sell—and sell quickly.

One who has loved much is forgiven much, said Christ.
Much must be forgiven Pound. Some of his hates were wit-
less, and some, in the context of contemporary history,
maleficent as well. His hate of Franklin Roosevelt was out
of all right proportion (even granting that Roosevelt used
an abominable English). When raging against Roosevelt,
whom he called "Old Sowbelly," Pound assumed a Jewish
accent (for some obscure reason) and actually bit his
thumb. He could and did talk for twenty minutes straight
on this subject. He told me that his hate for Roosevelt was
sufficient to dam up the Potomac River.

The bias against Jews is found here and there in *The Cantos*, and it came out often in his conversation at Saint Elizabeth's. However, Pound is far from the Nazi "Aryan supremacy" idea, with his Latin temperament, his devotion to the Oriental philosopher Confucius, and his championing of Leo Frobenius, who discovered ancient African Negro civilization. Pound's favorite German poet was Heine, a Jew (who often reminds one of Pound) of whom he wrote: "After Villon, the next poet with an absolutely clear palette is Heine." He translated Heine masterfully—eight poems remain in the present *Personae*—and addressed him in verse, using his Jewish rather than his Christian name:

> O Harry Heine, curses be,
> I lived too late to sup with thee!
> Who can demolish at such polished ease
> Philistia's pomp and Art's pomposities!

Some of Pound's judgments against Jewish culture have been made by Jews themselves; but having such ideas in the time of the Nazi persecution is, to say the least, bad timing. And though Pound had little in common with the Nazis (at Saint Elizabeth's he said "Hitler was hysterical"), he committed the great error of supporting the Axis side in the last war.

Another irony and paradox: "We always thought of him as *so* American," his English wife told me. "Violently American," Wyndham Lewis called him. Yet while at Saint Elizabeth's Pound was still under indictment for treason to the United States of America. And Pound's treason (if it was such) was impelled by an ardent patriotism—again paradoxically, that of an expatriate.

We must go back to Whitman to find a first-rate poet who feels "the American dream" as much as Pound. Yet *since* Whitman this country has moved far from the dream. Freedom of the press has lost much of its meaning when almost all newsstands are owned by one firm, which will stock only the hundred most popular—and vulgar— periodicals. Corporate consolidations continue, despite talk of free competition. The average citizen feels he has no influence on public affairs—and couldn't care less. Our democratic society is shot with the snobbery of social climbers. Pound quixotically hoped to bring the real and ideal Americas together again.

"Another struggle," he told the *Paris Review* interviewer, "has been to keep the value of a local and particular character, of a particular culture in this awful maelstrom, this awful avalanche toward uniformity. The whole fight is for the conservation of the individual soul." Hence, as an assertion of particularity, Pound loved dialect stories—and here again he goes against the present American grain. Now dialect jokes are taboo in the U.S. mass media, for fear a minority group will be offended; all must be steamrollered into uniformity, like the ground for the box houses in American suburbia.

In *The Cantos* and in person, Pound liked to tell dialect stories and would sometimes slip into American country speech, which he used amusingly. He himself was a subtle combination of rustic and cosmopolitan, and the mixture of rough and elegant diction gives much forcefulness to *The Cantos;* it is reminiscent of Shakespeare. At Saint Elizabeth's he seemed also a strange mixture of American and European. Even his speech showed a meld of American and British. When I first saw him in 1951, the British tones struck me. But the longer Pound stayed at Saint Elizabeth's, the more he spoke with an American accent.

American rusticism was perhaps a kind of self-assertion for Pound. At the same time, he was also a very cosmopolitan linguist. In 1915 he wrote that he knew "more or less of nine foreign languages." (The words "more or less" are typically candid.) But Pound had not studied his languages in a methodical schoolbook manner; he was never a person of routine, and I suppose little given to language-learning drudgery. While other students went for grammar, he went directly for the beauty and liveliness of the tongues he studied. His best languages were gotten by immersion in the speech. "It's good to be lazy," Pound told me. "A lazy man takes short cuts." However, even in the languages he was only scantily acquainted with, he acquired a choice vocabulary.

Pound had not an enormous amount of German, for example, but knew those earthy and direct expressions unique to German. In a letter to René Taupin (1928), mainly in French, he writes *"ich stamm aus Browning."* English equivalents—"I derive from Browning" or "I stem from Browning"—would not have conveyed genealogical descendence so concretely. At Saint Elizabeth's Pound told me, "I have read little German since Heine in the nineteen-tens." But later he read the memoirs of von Bülow and the second part of *Faust* in German, and told Omar Pound that *Faust II* is one of the books that a man can read each decade, learning more from it each time as he grows in wisdom himself. Pound read Leo Frobenius in French; his seven-volume edition of Frobenius' *Erlebte Erdteile* was thumbed only in the first chapters.

Italian, French, Spanish, and Latin he knew well. At Saint Elizabeth's he read Perez Galdos' *Doña Perfecta* and told me: "Modern Spanish is a better language for literature than modern Italian." His Greek was not large; it was mainly read with the help of the Loeb Classical Library translations. Nevertheless, in all English verse there is no better representation of the Greek way than in Cantos 2, 4, and 17. Far more than Keats and other Hellenizing romantic poets, Pound makes us feel how the Greeks perceived their gods.

Pound's Chinese was self-taught, and little. He knew enough to be able to piece out the Confucian texts with the help of English and French translations and commentaries. After I had studied Chinese for half a year at Harvard, that brilliant and brusque classical-Chinese scholar Achilles Fang, an admirer of Pound, approached me one day in the library and said, "Now you know more Chinese than Pound"—then strode off.

The scholars of Chinese at Harvard had differing opinions of Pound. Achilles Fang and Professor James Robert Hightower liked Pound's Chinese translations. Professor Francis Cleaves declared, with pleasant frankness, "I do not have a poetic soul," and said, "But how can Pound translate difficult Chinese poems if he knows hardly any Chinese?" I answered that poetry translation requires, most of all, knowledge of your own language and of people's hearts. Pound has an uncanny wisdom in both. His English vocabulary is vast and inventive. And his subtle comprehension of sentiments is marvelously shown by two poems of separation in *Cathay:* "Exile's Letter" and "The River Merchant's Wife." Moreover, Pound of course had help in his Chinese work: for *Cathay,* the Fenollosa manuscripts; for the Confucian texts, commentaries and translations in European languages; for *The Confucian Odes,* a Chinese-American lady who visited him regularly at Saint Elizabeth's to answer questions, plus other English translations of the Odes. Pound *has* "made these bones live." T. S. Eliot rightly called him "the inventor of Chinese poetry for our time."

The Cantos, allusive and multilingual, are an incitation to learning. It should not be supposed that the poet claims expertise in all the areas to which he refers and all the languages he cites. He simply wants the reader to be as curious as he himself has been. A passage from the *Thrones* section is illuminating:

> I shall have to learn a little greek to keep up with this
> but so will you, drratt you

Toward spelling, Pound had an Elizabethan indifference. I remember "trype!" and other unique Poundian spellings scribbled in the margin of a modern European history he passed on to me. (Since he had little space at Saint Elizabeth's, he would give his visitors books and magazines after he had finished reading them.) Pound's Greek orthography was abominable too. When *The Yale Poetry Review* published one of *The Pisan Cantos*, the editors gave the manuscript to a classics teacher for correction of spelling in the Greek citations, which was highly original.

Any story can be improved by putting it into verse, Pound had written. An important element of *The Cantos* is *talk;* Pound's ear for real speech is magnificent throughout. And his talk at Saint Elizabeth's was poetry—at least a rough draft of it. One cannot forget that grating voice, rhythmic and flexible, as it rose and fell, picked up volume and diminished, with the fine sense of drama and instinct for colorful facts. His speech got its impact from its terseness. The German word for poetry, *Dichtung*, means "condensation"—and Pound's speech and verse both had it to an extraordinary degree.

Perhaps Pound's political entanglements came from the fact that his mind simply stopped growing after 1920 or 1925. At Saint Elizabeth's one felt that he was changeless, an old rock over which the experiences of decades had washed. In the mid-fifties I mentioned to him the current revival of early music (which his own work on Vivaldi had anticipated), and he replied by speaking about Arnold Dolmetsch, maker of ancient instruments in London four decades before. Dolmetsch might have been the origin of this revival, he said. By this time, Pound's interest in early music seemed small; his past interest was sufficient for him. I suggested to Mrs. Pound that his friends present him with a phonograph and records of Lawes and Dowland, Renaissance composers celebrated in *The Cantos*. "It wouldn't be worth it," she said. "He would play them once and then give them away."

5

"What Does Mr. Pound Believe?"

Zenobia Jiménez, wife of the poet Juan Ramón Jiménez, complained to me: "When we visited Saint Elizabeth's Mr. Pound always talked as if we agreed with his political views. Often we did not." Jiménez, an exile from Franco Spain, was not likely, for example, to sympathize with praise of Mussolini. But this was Pound's attitude to nearly all his visitors—a genial assumption that they could not possibly think otherwise than he. Perhaps this was a way of converting his listeners, to bring them slowly around to his viewpoint. Or he may have tended to believe that no proper man could hold other views than his. Since he was generally well disposed toward his visitors, he assumed that they too were reasonable.

Marianne Moore writes: "Why cannot money and life go for beauty instead of for war and intellectual oppression? This question is asked more than once by the Cantos." Pound paradoxically believed in studying money so that people would be less materialistic—more inspired by the arts and less by Mammon. He felt that economies based on money-lending, as is ours, were inevitably hostile to the arts. Omar Pound explained his father's economic ideas in this way: "He is a sensitive person. During the First World

War, when he lived in England, some of his best friends were killed, men like Gaudier-Brzeska and T. E. Hulme, in whom he had great hopes. Wyndham Lewis was nearly killed. Why did all this waste happen? He brooded about it for years, and as a result took up Social Credit. He thought Social Credit would stop war."

Remembering Pound's hopes for Gaudier-Brzeska and Hulme, the restraint of these lines from *Hugh Selwyn Mauberley*, describing World War I, is even more poignant:

> There died a myriad
> And of the best, among them . . .

And several times in *The Cantos*, Pound quotes the painter Picabia, summarizing that holocaust with laconic eloquence: "Europe exhausted for the conquest of Alsace-Lorraine."

It is indeed a deep paradox that this ardent pacifist, a man bitter against war and militarism, was on the side of the aggressors in World War II. This may have been partly due to the stubbornness and confidence in his own views which had served so well in his efforts to reform English verse. After Mussolini attacked Ethiopia, allied himself with Hitler, and entered the war on Hitler's side, Pound was simply too fixed in his opinions to change. Mrs. Pound told me that when Italy invaded Ethiopia in 1936, Pound said to her he thought Mussolini had lost his feeling for the people (see "lost the feel of the people," Canto 86). Pound's basic faith in "the Boss" was apparently not shaken, however. I remember him at Saint Elizabeth's grimly showing his visitors photographs of Mussolini and mistress hung from the heels in the Milan square; and in *The Pisan Cantos* he calls Mussolini "the twice crucified" (referring to the fact that Mussolini was first shot and then hung up).

Pound's Rome Radio broadcasts seem even more naive in view of the fact that he actually had very little to do with the Fascist party or government in Italy. As witness to this, in 1948 some sixty citizens of Rapallo, headed by the mayor, signed the following statement:

> The undersigned, who knew the American writer Ezra Pound in Rapallo, where he had lived since 1923, declare it is not true that he took part in Fascist activities in this city. There is no record of his presence at local meetings, nor was he a member of Fascist organizations.
>
> He was always considered an American citizen, a friend of Italy, openly sympathetic with certain Fascist principles of a social-economic nature, and with the struggle against communism, which he believed was a danger to the United States themselves. During the war Mr. Pound continued to reside in Rapallo, and from his mode of life it was evident that he did not enjoy privileges, but that he even suffered hardships and economic privations.
>
> Since it is an evident fact that he never acted from motives of profit, he was able to keep the respect of even those neighbors of his who disagreed with his political opinions.
>
> During the long years of residence in Rapallo, Mr. Pound's activity was always artistic and cultural, as illustrated in his writings in literary criticism and political economy.
>
> He always conducted himself properly and never engaged in anti-Semitic activity.

Pound saw Mussolini only once—at the Palazzo Venezia in 1933—and in the first lines of Canto 41 he has left a record of their conversation:

"Ma questo,"
        said the Boss, "è divertente."
catching the point before the aesthetes had got there;

"But this is entertaining!" The Boss was referring to a copy of *A Draft of XXX Cantos* that lay on the desk before him; Pound had sent the book in as a preliminary to his visit. And the poet saw a profound meaning in Mussolini's casual comment: Mussolini, he thought, had realized that *The Cantos* were meant to give the reader pleasure rather than being a highbrow aesthetic business. In fact, Pound probably completely misunderstood the Boss—and it is a good indication of his naive attitude toward Fascism. Mussolini could read little English—surely not enough to understand *A Draft of XXX Cantos.* But he *had* to say something polite, and so he came out with "this is entertaining!" in much the spirit as when a lady relative of mine, to whom I presented my own poems, said "Oh, how nice!" because she didn't know what else to say.

Pound saw a virtue in the fact that Mussolini ruled directly. One knew who was responsible for what the government did, Pound said; there was no evasiveness. (He quoted Mussolini, in his own colorful translation: "We are tired of government in which there is no responsible person having a hind-name, a front name and an address.") Moreover, both Mussolini and Hitler denounced "international bankers," which jibed with Social Credit views. And it should not be forgotten that the local Fascist rule in a quiet and uneventful town on the Italian Riviera can hardly have been very nefarious.

At Saint Elizabeth's I asked Pound why he had approved of Mussolini's attack on France. "Well, Muss couldn't sit by and let Hitler take over *all* of Europe," he said. A strange reply! As if you saw a man burgling a house, and instead of trying to prevent him, joined the burglary!

However, any attempt to define Pound as a Fascist breaks down on the facts. Pound is simply too multifarious, too individual in his views. Archibald MacLeish said pointedly: "Certainly the *Pisan Cantos* are . . . in the very strict political sense of the term, pro-fascist—though I doubt myself very much that Pound *is* a fascist—or ever was. I think that his particular brand of political idiocy was of such a nature that the issues that the rest of us thought were around were irrelevant to him." Nilita Vientós once described Pound to me as an anarchist—and perhaps that label fits him as well as any. But he is always slipping in and out of labels.

Ostensibly Pound was unrepentant of his wartime broadcasts on Rome Radio, and asserted simply that he was trying to save the United States Constitution. "Free speech without free radio speech is zero," he would say at Saint Elizabeth's. He emphasized that he had to struggle to get permission from the Fascist authorities to make the broadcasts. "I kidnapped that microphone," he said often. Once he declared with an almost pitiful petulance: "The British warned Wodehouse to stop broadcasting for the Germans, and he did. *I* wasn't warned." When I asked Pound who had heard his broadcasts, he told me (aware of the irony, I think) "a couple of old ladies in Maine." Pound insisted that he had not spoken *for the Italians* but for himself—a tenuous distinction, and, whatever he may have thought, he placed himself in the position of supporting the Axis by appearing on Rome Radio.

A good instance of Pound's basic political naiveté—or at least of MacLeish's contention that his issues are not our issues—is his attitude toward Communism. For all his burning interest in politics, Pound had no strong opinions about Communism one way or the other. He simply disliked Russian things, for the Russian writers were generally too long-winded for him. Only Turgenev, the most European of the Russian novelists, met with his approval. So he was reluctant to concede that *anything* good could come out of Russia, including Communism.

At Saint Elizabeth's I tried to draw him out on this subject. His answers were vague and contradictory. "I have only met one Communist and he was a good guy," declared Pound. (The one Communist had come to see him in Rapallo.) And he said: "Marxism is a smokescreen. Marx did not understand the nature of money." Another time he spoke with approval of Mao Tse-tung because the Chinese Communists had nationalized banks. The fact was that Pound was so wrapped up in money economics that he had only rudimentary ideas about Communism.

"Anti-Semitic" is another label often applied to Pound. Especially after Hitler, this is a dirty word. One hesitates to use it about a man who maintains he is *not* anti-Semitic, and whose closest literary friend in the nineteen-thirties, the poet Louis Zukofsky, was a Jew. For years Pound wholeheartedly helped and encouraged Zukofsky, a younger and relatively unknown poet—and this at a time when he was raging against "the Jewish international banking ring!" Zukofsky wrote:

> I never felt the least trace of anti-semitism in his presence. Nothing he ever said to me made me feel the embarrassment I always have for the "Goy" in whom a residue of antagonism to "Jew" remains. If we had occasion to use the words "Jew" and "Goy" they were no more or less ethnological in their sense than "Chinese" and "Italian."

And Pound told Donald Hall in 1959: "If any man, any individual man, can say he has had a bad deal from me because of race, creed, or colour, let him come out and state it with particulars. The *Guide to Kulchur* was dedicated to Basil Bunting and Louis Zukofsky, a Quaker and a Jew."

The Jewish people who visited Pound at Saint Elizabeth's while I was there were treated with the same courtesy as other visitors. Pound told me that when he would expound his theories about "Jewish finance" to Zukofsky in the thirties, Zukofsky would quietly say: "I think we'd better not talk about that" (and I felt that Pound admired Zukofsky's restraint). "Anti-Semitism is a red herring," Pound said, and at Saint Elizabeth's he pointed out to me that there are no Jews in *The Cantos'* hell. Like Matthew Arnold—and even some Jewish writers, such as Simone Weil—Pound favored the Hellenic elements in Western culture as against the Hebrew. This intellectual position seems entirely tenable. But Pound went further. In his talk at Saint Elizabeth's (as well as occasionally in his writings), there was often a wild and quite unreasonable bias against Jews. For example, hearing him blame World War II on Morgenthau, Baruch, and Frankfurter (not on Hitler!), one was sure that here was a real mania. In his attitude toward individual persons, Pound was for the most part not anti-Jewish; in his ideas he certainly was.

I remember Pound greeting me at Saint Elizabeth's with "How's Weenie?" "*Who* is Weenie?" I answered—and it evolved that this was his word for the Jewish Supreme Court Justice Frankfurter. Since I rented a room in the home of a Jewish lawyer who was clerk to another Supreme Court Justice, Reed, Pound's wild disciple Mullins had told him I was (*ipso facto*) connected with the arch-villain Frankfurter. When I finally understood, I was furious, and said: "I have never met Justice Frankfurter but should be extremely honored to have the opportunity." Pound laughed, and for the rest of my visit tried to be conciliatory.

Nevertheless, it is mendacious to suggest that Pound abetted Eichmann, as Eric Bentley did in a letter to *The Reporter* magazine. If Pound (who surely had never even heard of Eichmann) is responsible for the death camps, then Bentley's idol Brecht is guilty of the kulaks' extermination, and by the same warped logic Bentley himself might take the blame for the slaughter of innocents at Hiroshima and Nagasaki. Bentley says that he is against Brecht's political views but admires him as an artist; he does not show the same tolerance to the artist Pound.

Pound the artist is in fact so multiform that a great variety of ideas may be found in *The Cantos*. It has been argued, with citations, that more of *The Cantos* is laudatory of Jews and Jewish things than hostile. Pound's traditionalism may please conservatives; leftists will enjoy the pungent attacks on big bankers and industrialists ("hoggers of harvest"). Pacifists will find many incisive anti-war passages in *The Cantos*. That poem exalts ideas of republican government; and has a good bit in support of aristocracy too. Hugh MacDiarmid the Marxist, Archibald MacLeish the liberal, and T. S. Eliot the conservative can all praise Pound's poetry *and* ideas, each from a different angle.

Pound is agnostic, or at least deist, in his religious attitude (like Confucius, he holds that we cannot understand the next world when we do not yet know this one). But religious people—especially Catholics—can find much congenial material in *The Cantos*. Pound looks upon the loss of reverence as one of our time's great losses. And no poet has conveyed as well as he the numinous reality of the Greek deities.

T. S. Eliot asked the famous question "What does Mr. Pound believe?" and this apparently rankled, because he tried to answer it on several occasions. Obviously Pound has a great number—perhaps an oversupply—of beliefs, but religious belief was what Eliot had in mind, and there Pound is eclectic, as he is in most areas. "The only chance for victory over the brainwash is the right of every man to have his ideas judged one at a time," he said. And the remark hits home.

This fundamental eclecticism, plus a deep-rooted respect

for others' opinions, may explain why Pound could maintain relations with a diversity of writers who had little or no contact with one another: Eliot, Hemingway, Yeats, Cummings, and Joyce, for example. It may be that *au fond* Pound is a great poet precisely because—as Eliot said of Henry James—he has a mind too fine to be trapped by ideas. Despite his economic theories, *things* are more important to Pound than ideas. Thus, whatever he treats he vivifies.

Was Pound in fact mad at Saint Elizabeth's? A Communist friend of mine at Harvard called him "mad like a fox." Some have suggested that the U.S. government arranged to have him declared insane in order to avoid the embarrassment of putting the country's leading poet on trial. Dr. Frederic Wertham wrote in a psychiatric journal: "Surely the psychiatrists know the difference between a political conviction and a delusion. . . . Ezra Pound has no delusions in a strictly pathological sense." Pound said at Saint Elizabeth's that the insanity ruling was an attempt to discredit his ideas ("so the young folks won't listen to grandpa"). Moreover, Pound declared that the government was afraid he would stand up in court and publicly "tell the truth about Roosevelt." A gentleman from India who visited Saint Elizabeth's said, when asked if Pound was crazy: "Yes, if he were not mad he could not endure with such serene courage his present environment."

I think that the judgment of insanity was not a "put-up job." It was made by four leading psychiatrists, from four different institutions, and I know no reason to suspect that they faked their report. Among other things, the shock of the war years and his mistreatment at Pisa must have done a destructive work on Pound's psyche. Douglass Paige wrote me: "E. P. used a vivid image to describe his mental condition in 1946: he said that it seemed as though a movie film were running through his head and that suddenly the film would jam and break, and then there would be only a white light."

However, the widely differing opinions and theories existing within psychiatry show us that this is far from an objective science. As the reader should realize by now, Pound showed no external sign of "insanity": had no tics, saw no ghosts, had no compulsive repeated movements. In fact, he appeared to be an extraordinarily sane and hearty human being, though a bit nervous, and his mind sometimes moved from subject to subject with a rapidity that confused the listener. But his ideas certainly were not normal.

Whether these ideas were any worse than those held by countless persons walking around outside insane asylums, the reader may decide. The worst of Pound's opinions, most people will think, is the anti-Jewish bias. In any case, Jews too read Pound's verse today and find it a source of delight and enlightenment—and the lives of both Jews and Gentiles will be enriched by his verse as long as English is read. If we blame Pound for being a "traitor," we might consider that another illustrious literary man, Dante, was believed a traitor by the Florentines—and now we remember Dante's poetry, not the treason. "The rest is dross."

Mr. Pound left Saint Elizabeth's still officially insane, released in the custody of his wife. He had lived through a time of cultural, moral, and social disintegration that made his own disintegration seem tiny. He told a reporter after his release: "No wonder my head hurts, all of Europe fell on it." Perhaps the best answer to the question of whether Pound was insane at Saint Elizabeth's is in the words crooned by Bing Crosby when I was a boy:

"All the monkeys aren't in the zoo."

6

Farewell

In June 1958 I was laboring as a galley slave for a New York City book publisher. A post card from Omar Pound announced he would be in the city that month and added: *"Confidentially,* I *may* be seeing a boat off—not a word to anyone, please!"* This cryptic note was my first indication that I would be seeing Ezra Pound in—of all strange places —New York City.

Two months before, the treason charge against Pound had been dismissed, on the basis that he would never be sane enough to stand trial. For ten years he had vigorously declined to accept a release from Saint Elizabeth's without a statement by the government (I believe he wanted the President himself to sign it) that Franklin Roosevelt had broken his oath of office to preserve the United States Constitution. Somehow he had become willing to abandon this demand. Representative Usher L. Burdick of North Dakota had called for Pound's release in a number of speeches in the House of Representatives. A flood of editorials in American publications—and especially in Italian journals—had advocated giving Pound his freedom. One article called Saint Elizabeth's "a closet which contains a national skeleton." Then Robert Frost came down to Washington and, as he put it, "sat in the Attorney General's office until he agreed that Pound could get out." "None of us can bear the disgrace of our letting Pound come to his end where he is," said Frost.

Thurman Arnold, "trust-busting" Assistant Attorney General of the United States under Franklin Roosevelt—now a member of the leading Washington law firm of Arnold, Fortas, and Porter—agreed to serve Pound without fee. On April 14, 1958, Attorney Arnold—representing Pound, he said, "at almost unanimous request of leading writers of the United States and England"—filed a motion in District Court for dismissing the treason charge. The motion stated: "If the indictment against him is not dismissed, he will die in Saint Elizabeth's Hospital. . . . There can be no benefit to the United States in maintaining him indefinitely as a public charge because that custody cannot contribute to his recovery and defendant's release would not prejudice the interests of the United States. The inevitable effect of failure to dismiss the indictment will be life imprisonment on account of alleged acts and events which can never be put to proof." United States government lawyers concurred, and on April 18 the indictment was dismissed by Judge Bolitha Laws, who twelve years before had presided at Pound's arraignment and trial.

During all these years Pound had never been alone; his only privacy had been a doorless cubicle. Save for two hours daily, madmen and guards were his only company. He had been convicted of no crime; he was undergoing no treatment at the hospital. And this treatment was accorded America's greatest poet.

The poet, now seventy-two years old, left Saint Elizabeth's and for the next months lived in and around Washington. Freedom! A splendid thing to enjoy in the spring!

It was assumed he would return to Italy, but I had not known when, nor where he would depart. Then on Sunday, June 29, Omar Pound appeared in New York City, and I learned that his parents had booked passage for Genoa on the *Cristoforo Colombo*, leaving from a West Side pier the next afternoon.

So that broiling hot June day I left my office at noon and stopped by a florist's to purchase a potted ivy plant; Pound—Antaeus—should not lose touch with the earth on his sea journey. Then I took a taxi to the pier. After wandering through corridors, as one often does on a strange ship, I found Pound's stateroom. A man stood by the door as if keeping watch—a newspaperman? a detective? I never found out. I knocked, Omar flung the door open, and a blast of air conditioning hit me.

I entered a room about fifteen feet by twenty, and there was Pound, reclining on a bunk in shorts, shirt front open, grizzled beard meeting grizzled chest foliage. He was smiling and jovial, but I sensed a restraint—probably tiredness or nervousness. Beside him sat Dorothy Pound, looking gray and happy, and Marcella Spann, a good-looking young schoolteacher who had visited him at the asylum, co-editor with him of the anthology *Confucius to Cummings*. On the other bunk were David Horton and wife, and two young men introduced as the Messrs. Sullivan.

It soon appeared that the Sullivans were total strangers to the Pounds—New York friends of Horton. Horton had crammed them into this tiny stateroom on the occasion of his farewell to the master. They had absolutely nothing to say. Pound scowled at them, and after a bit growled: "Now would Mr. Horton care to take the Sullivans *out?*" They leapt up, giggling inanely, and disappeared.

Horton was his usual scintillant self.

"How do you feel?" I asked Pound. "Well," he replied,

"there *is* a certain euphoria." Horton interrupted: "Aah
. . . aah . . . eu-*pho*-ria? . . . eu-PHO-ria? Wha—, wha's
that?" (For a decade at Saint Elizabeth's, Pound had been
patiently defining his words for Horton when requested.)
Pound did not answer.

"Would your publisher print *me?*" Pound asked, taunt-
ing me. "May be," I said. "Got anything?" "No, I'm dry as
a bone," he declared.

Pound spoke wittily of Fielding, whose merry spirit
seemed to fit his mood. To tease him, I inquired if he missed
Saint Elizabeth's. He replied with an apropos Jewish dialect
joke—not at all unfriendly to its protagonist, I remember.

After about twenty minutes, I took my leave of Olympus. I (poor devil) had to keep office hours, and this was
my lunch time. A few others came after I had departed:
Yale Professor Norman Holmes Pearson, Robert Mac-
Gregor of New Directions, and the Italian cultural attaché
in New York with his wife. The gathering was minimal.
Pound slipped out of New York as quietly as possible.

Mr. and Mrs. Pound had spent the preceding night in
Rutherford, New Jersey, with his friend of fifty-five years,
William Carlos Williams. From there, they went straight to
the ship. Sightseeing in New York seems to have had no interest for Pound.

PART THREE

Back to Italy

Pound sailed for Italy in high spirits; after all, a dream was coming true. But this time Italy perhaps did not meet his expectations.

The first two years were spent mainly with his daughter Mary at Schloss Brunnenburg, a castle perched on a mountain high over Merano in the Italian Tyrol. From his room in the tower he could see five castles; the Adige twists through the valley beneath. The weather is mild, as the valley opens to the south, the air crystal clear. Nearby are the castles of the troubadours Oswald von Walkenstein and Walther von der Vogelweide.

At Brunnenburg Pound saw few visitors because, Mrs. Pound told me, "He was so fed up with being surrounded by people at Saint Elizabeth's." At first Pound was delighted with the castle. "The perfect frame," he called it. He found wall space for his Gaudier-Brzeska drawings; Gaudier's bust of him stood in the garden facing east so that the first rays of morning sun touched it. He read *Uncle Remus* aloud to his two grandchildren at bedtime. He helped his daughter with her Italian translations of *The Cantos* and talked long with his son-in-law, Prince Boris de Rachewiltz, a noted scholar of Egyptian and African civilization. With saw and hammer, he made much of the furniture for his rooms at Brunnenburg (like Hans Sachs in *The Cantos*, "Schuhmacher und Poet dazu," he was handworker *and* poet). A handsome exhibition of his books and manuscripts was held in Merano. He read a good deal, including T. S. Eliot's later plays, and told Mrs. Pound he was astonished at how much mastery of technique had gone into their writing.

In Italy Pound composed Cantos 110 to 116, a superb summation of that mighty work. The note of humility and awakening from egoism, which had begun with the renowned "Pull down thy vanity" passage in *The Pisan Cantos*, is now more strongly emphasized. Cantos 115 and 116 are profoundly moving, two of the finest; they may have answered Eliot's criticism that Mr. Pound can see the hell in others but not in himself. Pound refers to this comment, I believe, in Canto 116:

> Many errors,
>   a little rightness
>   to excuse his hell and my paradiso

In the same Canto he says, presumably of himself and his verse:

> but the beauty is not in the madness
>   *   *   *
> and I cannot make it cohere
>   *   *   *
> To confess wrong without losing rightness
> Charity I have had sometimes,
>   I cannot make it flow through

And, to remind us that the poet is still the greatest in our language, he writes of himself in Canto 115:

A blown husk that is finished
                but the light sings eternal
a pale flare over marshes
   Where the salt hay whispers to tide's change

The Paris Review published an interview with him, made by Donald Hall in March 1959. In this splendid interview, distinguished by a new modesty and self-understanding, Pound admitted that Europe had been a disappointment to him. "The shock of no longer feeling oneself in the center of something is probably part of it," he said. And "there are so many things which I, as an American, cannot say to a European with any hope of being understood."

He went down to Rapallo in summer 1959, and there came the first break in his health. Severely ill, he was brought back to Brunnenburg in the back of a station wagon, then spent some time being treated at a Merano clinic. In December he traveled to Darmstadt, where he saw his Sophoclean *Women of Trachis* performed in a brilliant German translation of the English text by Eva Hesse (Kenneth Tynan wrote of the Berlin performance, "the tragedy came across like thunder"). Then, about the first of the year, he became ill again.

With the decline in his health, a strange thing happened, something one would hardly have expected: his self-confidence and élan broke too. He brooded and became increasingly uncommunicative. He gave up answering letters. He underwent an operation. He divided his time between Brunnenburg, Rapallo, and the tiny Venice apartment of his old friend Olga Rudge. He traveled twice to Rome, and was for a while in a Rapallo hospital. In March 1963 he gave an interview to the Italian magazine *Epoca* that showed an astonishing swing in a new direction. Among other things, he said:

I have lived all my life believing that I knew something. And then a strange day came and I realized that I knew nothing, that I knew nothing at all. And so words have become empty of meaning. . . .

It is something I have come to through suffering. Yes, through an experience of suffering. . . .

I have come too late to a state of total uncertainty, where I am conscious only of doubt. . . .

I do no work any more. I do nothing. I fall into lethargy, and I contemplate. . . .

Everything that I touch, I spoil. I have blundered always.

This was of course a complete reversal for him. Lifelong friends died one after another: Cummings and Aldington in 1962, Williams in 1963. And then in January 1965 the man whose poems Pound had discovered in London fifty years before, who had become England's most celebrated poet and dedicated his greatest work to Pound as "the better smith," T. S. Eliot, passed away. Olga Rudge took Pound to England, by airplane, for the memorial service in Westminster Abbey. England commemorated her dead poet with maximum solemnity, and in these magnificent surroundings Pound, who had been able to afford only a tiny triangular flat in Kensington while in England, paid his last respects to Eliot, who had lived no better in those times.

Pound stayed in England just two nights and a day—one night before the memorial service and one night after—and saw nobody except Mrs. Eliot. Faber and Faber, Eliot's publishers, arranged for Pound to enter the Abbey by a special side door, to preserve his privacy. Pound and Eliot had not seen each other since Pound was in Washington, as both had been rather immobile. Now, forty-four years after he had left England, Pound returned, to remember his friend. The trip was a great strain on him. As soon as he arrived home again, he reentered the Villa Chiara, a clinic in Rapallo.

For an Eliot memorial issue of the *Sewanee Review*, Pound contributed a brief note. No more moving memorial could have been composed.

> His was the true Dantescan voice—not honoured enough, and deserving more than I ever gave him. I had hoped to see him in Venice this year for the Dante commemoration at the Giorgio Cini Foundation— instead: Westminster Abbey. But, later, on his own hearth, a flame tended, a presence felt.
>
> Recollections? let some thesis-writer have the satis-faction of "discovering" whether it was 1920 or '21 that I went from Excideuil to meet a rucksacked Eliot. Days of walking—conversation? literary? le papier Fayard was then the burning topic. Who is there now for me to share a joke with?
>
> Am I to write "about" the poet Thomas Stearns Eliot? or my friend "the Possum"? Let him rest in peace. I can only repeat, but with the urgency of fifty years ago: READ HIM.
>
> E. P.

He missed the United States, wanted to see his birthplace Hailey. He bought airplane tickets to the United States for himself and Olga Rudge, then turned them in at the last moment. Summer 1965 found Pound in Spoleto for the Gian Carlo Menotti Festival, where his François Villon opera *The Testament* was performed as a ballet. A tall man, he now weighed ninety pounds. He traveled to Paris to examine proofs of the French review *L'Herne*, which was publishing a Pound issue. In the autumn he flew to Greece with Olga Rudge (his first visit there). He went to Athens and Delphi, saw the Castalian springs, and drank of them.

His eightieth birthday in October 1965 brought him a flood of congratulatory messages. A German television network photographed him at his home in Sant' Ambrogio overlooking the Mediterranean near Rapallo, among olives and eucalyptus trees. Pound was seen writing at his desk and strolling through his garden, deep in thoughts, as the announcer read the plangent lines from Canto 116, a summation and valedictory:

> I have brought the great ball of crystal,
> who can lift it?
> Can you enter the great acorn of light?

The Cantos—"the great ball of crystal"—were complete. The rest is up to the reader.

Pound would not speak for the television. Toward the end of the broadcast he was seen full length, very thin, standing facing the photographer, chin up. The camera swung nearer and nearer to the poet until only his face was seen, and finally, for about ten seconds, a single burning eye.

I saw him in Merano after his return to Italy. One fine autumn day in 1960, my wife and I drove through the rolling countryside of southern Bavaria, then up 6000 twisting feet across the Passo Giovo into country bare of trees, and down into the mild southward-facing valley that holds Merano. Mist-covered mountains shoulder up on two sides, and the air has a mountain cleanliness. The townspeople are part Tyrolean German, part Italian. It is a town of cafés and churches, old gates and curving streets.

Schloss Brunnenburg stands on a mountainside commanding a vast view of Merano and the valley. From it you can see perhaps twenty miles. We parked our car in Dorf Tyrol, a village above Merano, and villagers pointed out the Schloss, some hundred yards below the road: a small turreted castle, seen in dizzying perspective against the valley beneath.

So we walked down an earthen path, through fruit orchards, toward the Schloss. Later we learned that all the castle's provisions came down this path on donkey back. There was no telephone. Arriving at the castle, we swung open a great wooden gate, and shouted up a rampart. From a high window peeped the head of a lady, who soon appeared at the rather shabby door before us: Pound's daughter Mary, a graceful lady in her thirties with a round, girlish Irish-type face. Up a winding staircase, and there was Mrs. Pound. For a moment we chatted with her in a stony room. Then: "Shall I fetch Ezra? He is resting in his room upstairs." And she departed.

We looked around us. The room is fantastic; outside of art museums, I have seen nothing like it. Dark wood paneling, stone, a few old chairs, heavy but elegantly shaped, and a few pieces of sculpture—African and Egyptian. In an alcove toward the valley, benches are built into the wall and there is a table. Beyond, a vertiginous view of the valley alive with sunlight.

He appeared smiling at the door—tall but a bit stooping, more wrinkled, tangly beard whiter—and shambled to the alcove where we were. There he pulled up a chair and sat facing the great valley. I seated myself on a bench and we talked, while Mrs. Pound departed with my wife for a tour of the castle. We spoke of common American friends—the sculptor Michael Lekakis and the composer Frank Moore. He seemed very tired, at times had difficulty finishing a sentence, at times almost whispered. "I've been sick, you know," he said. "I haven't been able to read for a year." "In any case, you are resting," I said hopefully. "No . . . just . . ." his voice trailed away ". . . pushing."

I told him of my Greek translations, and he said, "With Greek . . . I never got over . . . the difficulty . . . of learning the alphabet." A strange excess of modesty! Pound has changed considerably. He is much slower, and seems unsure of himself.

Mrs. Pound returns with my wife. She says that in the past years their only visitors have been Frank Moore and a young American scholar who has settled in the town and regularly interviews Pound. The poet lives in a stone room at the very top of the castle—up eighty-four spiral stairs, I learn later—so high that sometimes a strong wind smashes a window. Schloss Brunnenburg, Mrs. Pound tells us, was built as a barracks for a larger castle we can see up the mountain. It is twelfth-century. Cloud shadows shift over the valley.

Pound speaks irritably of the fact that Karl Shapiro has recently attacked him as Fascist and anti-Semite. These charges are unjust, he feels. "Someone is needed to defend grandpa," he says.

In *Personae* he writes "old friends the most." Now Mrs. Pound amiably tries to establish an ancient history for our acquaintance, which really is relatively recent. "Let's see, Reck; we've known you for a long time. Why, it's been . . . it's been . . . *ten years* now."

As we stand up to take our leave, Pound rises suddenly and, with an access of vigor, *kicks* his chair back. We shake hands in farewell. And the dear old face, seamed with seventy-five years of struggle for excellence, crinkles profoundly in a smile.

Later I recorded the visit in a poem:

EZRA POUND'S

eye
rinsed the interlocutor.
He announced, "I

haven't been able to read
for a year."
"But resting?"

"No, just
pushing."
Oh, unending

battle against bunkum
intermitted,
lull

in storm. Stars
shine and the ascetic tosses,
tosses on his bed of nails.

From her tour of the castle with Mrs. Pound, my wife remembers drawings of Wyndham Lewis and a sculpted Gaudier-Brzeska cat. As they walked down a stony deserted hall, with windows opening on a medieval courtyard, my wife inquired if the castle was cold in wintertime.

And that gracious lady of breeding, her face still a cameo, leaned to my wife and said in a stage whisper, with a mischievous little girl's smile:

"*DAMN* COLD!"

Pound's Venice apartment is on a tiny side street very near the end of the twisty Grand Canal, in the section called San Gregorio. Not far off is Peggy Guggenheim's home and art museum. Across the Grand Canal: Hemingway's old haunt, the posh Gritti Palace Hotel. Fifty yards from Pound's apartment, the Grand Canal meets the sea, and there is the ancient customs house, the Dogana di Mare:

> I sat on the Dogana's steps
> For the gondolas cost too much, that year,
>   [Canto 3]

On September 28, 1966, I saw Pound again, in Venice. It was a clammy day of sirocco, that moist wind which blows up from Africa and sets the Venetians complaining. Sunlight filtered through haze. I arrived in San Gregorio early, sat for a while watching the gondolas pitch wildly on the Grand Canal, then knocked on Pound's door. It was opened by Olga Rudge, a white-haired lady with finely cut features, looking remarkably like her daughter Mary. A violinist, she had been Pound's friend since the nineteen-twenties. The apartment, it seemed, consisted of three small rooms, each a separate story. Olga Rudge immediately sat me down and explained what I more or less knew already: Ezra speaks little, and does not answer letters. She remembered I had written him on his eightieth birthday, and said he was grateful for it. But Pound's interlocutors should not think that his silence means unfriendliness or indifference, Olga Rudge said. He in fact listens carefully to every word, and very occasionally makes a remark that shows how closely he is attending. She cited his comment on a performance of *The Winter's Tale* by the Edinburgh Festival Company, which they had recently seen in Venice: "ham and beatnik."

Having finished this forewarning, she led me upstairs. In his third-floor room, there he sat. I was prepared for the thinness by photographs I had seen. He smiled, tight-lipped, beneath his wispy white beard, looked very attentive, and said nothing. I talked to him, and with Olga Rudge. He watched me with piercing eyes, in a kindly way, occasionally smiling a bit when the talk took a humorous turn. After about five minutes, he still had not spoken a word. There was a pause in the conversation, and he said to me—suddenly and quite clearly—"You were in Japan, weren't you?" and after I had answered, "Where were you born?" Then silence again. Olga Rudge had warned me that I should not try to interrogate him, as it would be useless. When I did put a direct question to him, he would not reply, or his lips would move as if he were trying to form an answer, but the answer would not come. His hands were raw with eczema, and he scratched them nervously.

Olga Rudge went downstairs, and I talked to Pound but not with him. Then all of a sudden he said, referring to Olga Rudge—rather abruptly, as I had not been speaking of her: "She has an enormous courage."

"So do you," I said.

"Not like hers," said Pound.

Olga Rudge returned and suggested that we go out to lunch. Pound rose with energy, grasped his walking stick firmly, and down the stairs we went and out onto the Zattere, the promenade that runs along the very wide Canale della Giudecca. Across the canal, in haze, the dream-like churches and palazzi of La Giudecca. Pound strode forward without feebleness; he did not talk. After a few minutes' walk on the Zattere, through misty sunlight, we turned down a side street, and Olga Rudge pointed out to me the house where Pound had lived when he came to Venice in 1908 and published *A Lume Spento*. Across the street there was still a gondola repair shop; before it, gondolas lay in drydock. After more than half a century Pound had returned to live in the same neighborhood, had so to speak come full circle.

We walked down the Fondamenta Eremite, the canal water lapping pleasantly at our side, and entered the Trattoria Montin, where, Olga Rudge said, she and Pound often dine. It has been frequented by artistic people since D'Annunzio made it his eating place. We were served a fine Venetian dinner, and Pound sat wordless while Olga Rudge and I conversed. We discussed Denis Roche's mistranslation of *The Cantos'* line "O lynx, keep the edge on my cider"; Roche had rendered "edge" as "borde." And abruptly as ever Pound broke his silence and said (showing that he had by no means lost his feeling for the *mot juste*), "By edge I meant 'tang.'" I mentioned that I was told he had not liked Eustace Mullins' biography of him. He said, "Mullins has a sense of humor. He should not be condemned for that." From all I have heard about him, Pound has become less and less bitter, less ready to condemn.

That evening I dined with Pound and Olga Rudge at a pension near their home. Daniel Cory, Santayana's literary executor, appeared with his wife, and he and I talked about metrics while the greatest metrical inventor in twentieth-century English verse sat there hunched and silent. All our attempts to draw him into the conversation failed.

After dinner I accompanied him and Olga Rudge to their door. Pound turned away with no farewell, not noticing the hand I offered. In general, I received a curious impression. It often seemed as though *il miglior fabbro* was paying close attention to what went on about him and perhaps wished to communicate more but could not. At the same time, however, I thought that at least part of him was in quite another world. Was this the result of his long voyage seeking wisdom, or simply of illness? I do not know.

PART FOUR

The Meaning of Pound

I

A Universal American

An aspect of Pound's greatness most appropriate to this century is his international spirit. The world, it has been alleged, is shrinking; an examination of airline timetables would seem to confirm this. More than any other author, Pound is international. His vital interests extend from Greece westward to Italy, France, England, Spain, Africa (through Frobenius), America, Japan, and China. One of the reasons his verse is renowned and prized over the world is just this internationality. When Omar Pound was traveling across north India, he stopped at Santiniketan, a university in Bengal founded by Rabindranath Tagore. There white-robed students showered him with detailed questions about *The Cantos*—many of which, to his embarrassment, he could not answer.

Pound prized contacts between cultures. "The most interesting Englishmen are the ones born in India," he told René Laubiès at Saint Elizabeth's. But international*ism* as an abstract idea did not appeal to Pound. In all, he preferred concrete things, particulars, and therefore he loved particular civilizations only. Since cultural internationalism is expressed largely by the dissemination of Coca-Cola and rock 'n' roll, on one side, and compulsory Marxist study on the other, Pound's feelings are understandable.

When Pound talked about the United Nations at Saint Elizabeth's, he generally slandered it. So I was touched to hear about an act of generosity, which may have moved Pound too. Dag Hammarskjöld, then UN Secretary General, somehow learned that Pound was reading the botanist Linnaeus, Hammarskjöld's countryman and founder of modern scientific classification. Hammarskjöld was large enough to forgive Pound's attitude to the UN, if he knew of it. He sent the poet a copy of a speech he had given on Linnaeus, with a friendly note. And, speaking at the New York City Museum of Modern Art in October 1954, the Secretary General said eloquently:

> Modern art teaches us to see by forcing us to use our senses, our intellect, and our sensibility, to follow it on its road of exploration. It makes us seers—seers like Ezra Pound when, in the first of his Pisan Cantos, he senses "the enormous tragedy of the dream in the peasant's bent shoulders." Seers—and explorers—these we must be if we are to prevail.

One of Pound's visions was that the meeting of East and West might be consummated. During his confinement at Saint Elizabeth's this matter occupied him intensely. He translated Sophocles' *Trachiniae* with a dedication expressing the hope that it might be performed in the Japanese Noh theater. (It has not yet been.) He put the oldest Chinese classic, *The Book of Songs*, into a very modern English. He studied Philostratus' *Life of Apollonius of Tyana* because he saw the first marriage of East and West in Apollonius, a neo-Pythagorian who traveled to India in the first century A.D. Apollonius appears variously in the *Rock Drill* part of *The Cantos*. I remember, too, Pound's delight when the Greek poet Zesimos Lorenzatos translated his

Cathay into modern Greek; he proudly showed the volume to visitors at Saint Elizabeth's. Lorenzatos had brought China to Greece. Pound dreamed of a world culture founded on these two.

Pound cultivated a cosmopolitan, universal spirit *and* his Americanism at the same time. Through all the decades in Europe, he tried to keep his American roots—and succeeded better than many good poets who stayed at home. His poetry often shows a marvelous command of real American speech, as it rolls off the tongue, not as pedants write it. Sometimes, in the effort of self-assertion, he even overdoes his Americanism a bit, as in Canto 12: "Go to hell Apovitch, Chicago ain't the whole punkin." The problem of his own national identity surely troubled Pound. "A man who fits into his milieu as Frost does is to be considered a happy man," he told Donald Hall in 1959. Part of Henry James' fascination for him must have been his attempt, through the expatriate James, to discover himself as an American living abroad.

As an expatriate, Pound's attitude toward his homeland was equivocal. He criticized Americans for not being American enough, according to his ideal of America. And, though he condemned American "petty optimism"—declaring that he would believe in America when it produced a real honest pessimistic writer, not just a literary one—we find him increasingly falling into the same error for which he attacks his countrymen. He was actually a born optimist, like most Americans. In *The Cantos* he several times quotes Turgenev that nothing is incurable except death. He came to believe that the application of money to writers could cure even bad writing—of course a colossal oversimplification. The peak of his optimism was reached in the nineteen-thirties, when he tried single-handedly to "save Europe by economics." *That* fond dream had its apocalyptic ending in the war. In any case, Pound's native hopefulness may have helped him survive the hellhole of Saint Elizabeth's. There he liked to tell the tale of the Philadelphia frog who, having fallen into a pail of milk, croaked "Ah me, I sink," and sank; while the Chicago frog, in the same predicament, croaked "Gotta get out, gotta get out," kept on kicking till he had churned the milk to butter, and hopped out.

Archibald MacLeish pointed out that Pound's vital interests in various cultures—what MacLeish calls his "cross-fertilizing, dragging things in"—is in itself American. "We're interested in other people, we're interested in various chains and veins and derivations," said MacLeish. "Europeans are inclined to let well enough alone and to assume that each culture belongs to itself, and one culture is enough for any man to bother about." Hence the paradox: because Pound is so international, he is so American. MacLeish also sees Pound's "economic and political immaturity" as American. "There's a kind of naïve rushing into areas that wiser men would try to know a little more about before they enter which is rather characteristic of American writers," MacLeish says.

Pound's attitude toward democracy separated him from most of his countrymen intellectually. Like that other very American writer, H. L. Mencken, he didn't believe in it—or at any rate, didn't swallow it whole. "There is no democracy in the arts," Pound wrote Amy Lowell, and he asked: "Is it that real democracy can exist only under feudal conditions, where no man fears to recognize creative skill in his neighbor?" He was attracted to aristocracy, as it had managed culture in some of its greatest ages, and made an acute distinction between aristocracy and snobbishness: "Aristocracy decays when it ceases to be selective, when the basis of selection is not personal. It is a critical acuteness, not a snobbism, which last is selection on some other principle than that of a personal quality. [Snobbism] is servility to rule-of-thumb criteria, and a dullness of perception, a timidity in acceptance. The whole force of the Renaissance was in the personality of its selection."

In politics as well as in the arts, Pound did not favor mass rule. For one thing, he believed it led to the "retrocession of power," where the real power is held by a few who manipulate the masses. Also he saw that modern mass societies are not noted for favoring the arts (and "cultural explosions" are dangerous as other explosions).

However, Pound wanted not tyranny or autocratic government (despite his support of Mussolini, the reasons for which are somewhat another story), but republican government as it existed in the years just after the American republic was founded—a Quixotic ideal! At Saint Elizabeth's he would advocate broadcasting of Congressional sessions, so that people would know better what was really happening in public affairs; he hated behind-the-scenes manipulation of all kinds. And liberty of expression was extremely important to Pound. He liked to quote from Rémy de Gourmont's letter to him: "to express frankly what one thinks—sole pleasure of a writer." Unlike Sholokhov, Neruda, and other Communist writers, Pound never advocated suppression of opinion of any kind.

Pound is, in fact, a thoroughgoing American—by birth and conviction. Perhaps this is clearest to Englishmen; Wyndham Lewis, Ford Madox Ford, and Dorothy Pound have all testified that they found him quintessentially American. His credo of "make it new"—that constant intellectual forging forward—is merely the American frontier-opening spirit put into the world of letters. And if we Americans have any national philosophy or way of looking at things, it is pragmatism, the idea that practical usability is what counts. In his attitude to the arts, Pound developed a very American philosophy of his own, an exalted pragmatism. Beauty for him has a purpose: "it reminds one what is worth while." Art "gives data for ethics," it "trains the muscles." In *How to Read*, he defined the practical purpose of literature:

> Has literature a function in the state, in the aggregation of humans, in the *res publica* . . . ? It has.
>
> And this function is *not* the coercing or emotionally persuading, or bullying or suppressing people into the acceptance of any one set or any six sets of opinions as opposed to any other one set or half-dozen sets of opinions.
>
> It has to do with the clarity and vigour of "any and every" thought and opinion. It has to do with maintaining the very cleanliness of the tools, the health of the very matter of thought itself. . . . The individual cannot think and communicate his thought, the governor and legislator cannot act effectively or frame his laws, without words, and the solidity and validity of these words is in the care of the damned and despised *litterati*. When their work goes rotten—by that I do not mean when they express indecorous thoughts—but when their very medium, the very essence of their work, the application of word to thing goes rotten, i.e. becomes slushy and inexact, or excessive or bloated, the whole machinery of social and of individual thought and order goes to pot.

Because Pound wanted poetry to fulfill this social function, he demanded that it fit the facts, was opposed to everything highfalutin in it. "Poetry should be as well-written as good prose," he declared again and again, and wrote: "All good art is realism of one kind or another." Pound despised unrestrained emotionality, and he is at his humorous bitterest when attacking A. E. Housman for claiming that good poetry cuts loose from the intellect —*that* idea is "bathos, slop, ambiguity, word-twisting," declares Pound.

Good hard-headed American principles! And yet we find him writing Kitasono Katue: "I dunno what my 23 infantile years in America signify. I left as soon as [my] motion was autarchic." *I* know.

2

Maintain Antisepsis

pity, yes, for the infected
                         but maintain antisepsis,
let the light pour.
                         [Canto 94]

At Saint Elizabeth's Pound irritated me by declaring that
his poem "Hugh Selwyn Mauberley" is merely a popularized version of his "Homage to Sextus Propertius." I
thought "Mauberley" his best earlier poem—and many
critics agreed, even those hostile to the rest of the *Personae*,
like F. R. Leavis. Parts of "Mauberley" are so difficult you
would hardly think of it as *popularized!*

Now I can better see why Pound preferred "Propertius." That poem has a total music of attitude and rhythm
which renders precisely a composite Pound–Propertius—
Pound in the mask of Propertius—whose light-hearted
irony both covers and expresses amorous passion, a tragic
sense of transitoriness, and savage indignation at pomp and
official stupidity. The peculiar rhythm of the long lines—
free-running and clean-cut—represents the gay, free, stoic
character of Pound–Propertius himself. *"Propertius,"*

Pound has written, defines "a relation to life." "*Mauberley* is a mere surface," the poet wrote Felix Schelling. "Propertius" is "Mauberley" in depth.

The center of *Propertius*' attack is stuffiness. Pound's profound dislike for stodginess and cant runs all through *The Cantos;* it is one of his real contributions to English literature. Considering this aversion, even something like the wild Tale of the Honest Sailor (Canto 12) has its place in *The Cantos.* This fine dirty joke is told by the bored Jim X at a bank directors' meeting (notice how Pound keeps almost hypnotically repeating the word *bored*, to emphasize how *thoroughly* bored Jim is). The point of the story is that Jim is shaking up the stuffed shirts.

In "Propertius" Pound is remaking our attitudes toward the classics, teaching us to walk familiarly with them. There is a classicism as false as *chinoiserie* is in relation to real Chinese art: handsome semi-naked men and women uttering pompous platitudes, like Tennyson's Vergil, who uttered "the stateliest measure ever moulded by the lips of man." "Propertius" sweeps away this fakery as Pound makes one classic alive and up-to-date. Pound wrote:

> The one use of a man's knowing the classics is to prevent him from imitating the false classics.
> You read Catullus to prevent yourself from being poisoned by the lies of pundits; you read Propertius to purge yourself of the greasy sediments of lecture courses on "American literature," on "English Literature from Dryden to Addison," you (in extreme cases) read Arnaut Daniel so as not to be over-awed by a local editor who faces you with a condemnation in the phrase "paucity of rhyme."
> The classics, "ancient and modern," are precisely the acids to gnaw through the thongs and bull-hides with which we are tied by our schoolmasters.

> They are the antiseptics. They are almost the only
> antiseptics against the contagious imbecility of man-
> kind.

So we find Pound taking his stand with the classics "made
new." Like Confucius, he calls himself a transmitter not a
creator.

Pound's antipathy to cant made him hate "artiness."
Achilles Fang once said to me, neatly: "Pound is for the
artisans, not the arty boys." Writing, to Pound is a craft.
And he tried to teach that craft. So we have still another
paradox: Pound, who seems thoroughly unacademic, is in
fact quite didactic—and perhaps academic in the best sense,
because he teaches the enthusiasm for knowledge as well as
the knowledge itself. "The most contagious teacher I have
ever known," Marianne Moore called him.

The young people always interested Pound the teacher
most. He wrote Harriet Monroe: "I don't lay as much
stock by teachin' the elder generation as by teachin' the
risin'." Countless writers sought his opinion of their own
work over half a century, and he gave it generously. Pound
had the rare tact and genius to realize that a critic must not
try to stamp his subject in his own image. He said: "It is
nearly impossible to make the RIGHT suggestion for
emending another man's work. . . . At most one can put
one's finger on the fault and hope the man himself will receive inspiration from the depths of his own personal
Helicon."

Much of Pound's verse too is deliberately didactic. He
felt that aestheticism had gone as far as it could in poetry.
"To hell with cookie-pushers who think poetry is a bun
shop and are busy making eclairs," he declared in 1956—a
remark reminiscent of Kierkegaard's comment that philosophy is not one of the bonbons of life.

Pound wanted to put ideas over, and he often had to
fight to do it. But his aggressiveness had the amiable feature

that he could take criticism as well as deliver it. I think he never dropped a friend because the friend criticized him— and many did, with acerbity: Aldington, Lewis, Williams, Eliot. In the *Letters* we even find Pound needling his friend Edgar Jepson for sparing him in a general condemnation of American poets: "Also, mon ami, most of my stuff must upset you nearly as much as Masters, don't let's beat about the bush, not that bush at any rate"—which sportsmanship is surely an aspect of greatness. Only once, it seems, did Pound let an attack get under his skin—Professor Hale's pedantic criticism of "Propertius"—and then, in his reply to Hale, Pound left not a hair unscorched.

Pound studied fencing when he was at college and prac- ticed it through several decades—and perhaps this helps ex- plain something of his poetic and critical style. Pound is light, elegant, moves gracefully, and when he finds the *mot juste*, deftly touches the point as no other writer does.

However, he at times cultivated a violence of expression that is no credit to him. The *Atlantic Monthly* may have committed vast sins, but it is childish to express a desire to shoot the editor. Pound had a tendency to regard people as either angels or devils. Even in his judgment of one individ- ual's qualities, he often saw either dark black or bright white. He writes that Swinburne's biographer Edmund Gosse was "a silly and pompous old man" who had fulfilled the functions of one official position "with great credit and fairness," had acquired from the great Victorians "only the cant and the fustiness," and had "written one excellent novel"—the good-bad pendulum swinging back and forth so violently that we wonder how all these opposite qualities can belong to one man.

At worst, Pound's criticism has too much of "I do not think it possible to overemphasize . . ." and "I cannot re- peat too often that . . ." Then he will candidly add in a later edition—instead of simply emending the text—"this

earlier opinion of mine now appears to me gross exaggeration." But perhaps we should allow Pound some colorful
overstatement. Reading him we are never bored.

Pound had a sportsmanship and selflessness that enabled
him to work *with* other poets to a remarkable degree; there
is surely no parallel to it in the literary life of our century.
He taught and learned from Hulme, Yeats, Eliot, Williams,
and possibly Cummings. The interaction of Eliot and
Pound is intricate, fascinating to observe. Consider the influence of the early Cantos (1917–1919) on Eliot's *The
Waste Land* (1921), the same kind of thesaurus of fragments. Consider, too, that "The Love Song of J. Alfred
Prufrock" (1917) must have shown the way for Pound's
"Hugh Selwyn Mauberley" (1920); both are poems of self-
description through a mask of irony. Eliot wrote that in his
early days he had to exercise great restraint not to compose
lines of verse too reminiscent of Pound's. Williams and
Pound probably also taught each other. Did Williams help
keep Pound from becoming an exotic? Did Pound fix Williams' attention on craftsmanship? In any case, during this
century of literary solipsism, it is remarkable to find a
writer so able to work with other writers as Pound.

Excesses and strangeness in Pound's thought are often
explicable as counteraction: he may be understood as an
antibody for some of our worst diseases. To an age that
cloaks materialism by a sham idealism, Pound presents the
reverse. Calling himself a plain man of facts, he acts the
part of a materialist. Yet an untrumpeted idealism underlies
all his writing.

To a people eroded by cynicism, Pound offers conviction, enthusiasm, and reverence. (In fact, enthusiasm—
considered in its root meaning of "being inspired or pos-
sessed by the god"—is a kind of reverence.) "The states
have passed thru a dam'd supercilious era," Pound quotes
his friend Congressman Tinkham in *The Pisan Cantos*. And

in the *Paris Review* interview, he says, "People who have lost reverence have lost a great deal."

In his demand for particularization and precision of expression, Pound also offers an antidote to an illness that kills much writing nowadays: use of pompous abstractions. Malcolm Cowley inaccurately summarized Pound's opposition to abstraction as the demand that you say "carrots, peas, spinach, and lettuce" instead of "vegetables." "Vegetables" at least has a clear denotation. Pound told Donald Hall: "You never get clarity as long as you have these package words, as long as a word is used by twenty-five people in twenty-five different ways." When we use such words, we are fooling ourselves.

At Saint Elizabeth's Pound would offer writers a bit of advice he had picked up from Ford Madox Ford: "Get a dictionary and learn the meanings of words." You can just look around to see the crime this advice should prevent— logocide, word murder. Pound rightly thought that if words are not used properly, a civilization rests on an insecure base.

Yet Pound, though he understood and fought our time's moral and linguistic disorder, could not conquer the disorder within himself. This is the tragedy of Pound, and prevents *The Cantos* from taking a place beside *The Iliad* and the *Divina Commedia*. At least we may say that *The Cantos* still serve a purpose in combating our confusion because their own disorder is different from the times'.

I remember asking Pound when *The Cantos* would end. He said only that he wanted to write more cantos than Dante. I admired the *brio* of this reply, but a firm principle of poetic organization seemed lacking. Basically the fault may be with the disordered times, not Pound. Might any large-scale organization in verse now lack a correlative in society, and therefore be superficial?

3

A Genius at Work

The finest achievement of Pound's intercultural labors, in which centuries and vast distances are instantly spanned by a brilliant act of imagination, is his linking of East and West.

His adaptations of Ernest Fenollosa's Chinese poetry manuscripts, first published in 1915 as *Cathay* and now printed in *Personae*, are justly popular. T. S. Eliot called them "translucencies." Ford Madox Ford was especially fond of the "Exile's Letter," and declared *Cathay* "a beautiful book," while "The River Merchant's Wife" has been loved by great numbers of readers, as witness its presence in so many American poetry anthologies. But how much of these superb translations is Pound's work and how much Fenollosa's?

I was privileged to examine the Fenollosa manuscripts at Schloss Brunnenburg—about a dozen schoolboy-type notebooks with penciled entries, now fading, in a handsome flowing hand. These contain notes on magazine articles about Far Eastern subjects, lecture notes from the Tokyo University classes in Far Eastern literature that Fenollosa attended, Fenollosa's essay "The Chinese Written Character as a Medium for Poetry," and the draft translations of

Chinese poetry and Japanese Noh drama. The answer to the question of how much Pound contributed to the final versions is: an extraordinary amount! Pound worked a miracle in turning Fenollosa's sprawling lines into a coruscant and durable poetry, without sacrificing their sense. His contribution was also one of selection; Fenollosa's notebooks contain, for example, twenty-seven poems by Rihaku (Japanese pronunciation of Li Po), only nine of which appear in *Cathay*.

Pound's reworking must have been facilitated by the fact that the Fenollosa notebooks are arranged in a very orderly manner. The Chinese poems are all five characters to a line. Fenollosa gives first the phonetic transcription of each line (in Japanese pronunciation of the Chinese characters), then a character-by-character translation, and finally a translation of the line as a whole. Pound relied most on the latter for his own versions.

Among the nine Li Po poems which Pound presents in *Cathay* are the "River Merchant's Wife" and the "Exile's Letter." I copied Fenollosa's renditions of the renowned "River Merchant's Wife" and the moving end of the "Exile's Letter," taking down the phonetic transcription and the character-by-character translation only when it appeared that Pound used them in his final version. It is extremely instructive to observe what Pound did to the Fenollosa drafts; we are watching a genius at work.

Here are the last lines of "Exile's Letter," in which a man is writing a dear friend from whom he has long been separated:

The Fenollosa original:

> (If you) ask me how much I regret the parting
> I would answer that my sorrow is as much as the falling
>   flowers of spring

Struggling [?] with one another in a tangle.
Words cannot be exhausted
Nor can the feelings be fathomed
So calling to me my son I make him sit on the ground for
     a long time
And write to my dictation
And sending them to you over a thousand miles we think
     of each other at a distance.

The Pound version:

And if you ask how I regret that parting:
It is like the flowers falling at Spring's end
         Confused, whirled in a tangle.
What is the use of talking, and there is no end of talking,
There is no end of things in the heart.
I call in the boy,
Have him sit on his knees here
         To seal this,
And send it a thousand miles, thinking.

"The River Merchant's Wife" presents a tender picture
of a childish heart—one of the loveliest poems in English.

The Fenollosa original:

My hair was at first covering my brows (child's method
     of wearing hair)
Breaking flowers I was frolicking in front of our gate
When you came riding on bamboo stilts (you—ride on—
     bamboo horse—come)
And going about my seat you played with the blue plums
Together we dwelt in the same Chokan Village
And we two little ones had neither mutual dislike nor sus-
     picion.

The Pound version:

While my hair was still cut straight across my forehead
I played about the front gate, pulling flowers.
You came by on bamboo stilts, playing horse,

You walked about my seat, playing with blue plums.
And we went on living in the village of Chokan:
Two small people, without dislike or suspicion.

The Fenollosa original:

At fourteen I became your wife.
Bashful, I never opened my face (I never laughed)
But lowering my head I always faced toward a dark wall
ashamed to see anybody (she sat in dark corners)
And though a thousand times called, not once did I look
around.

The Pound version:

At fourteen I married My Lord you.
I never laughed, being bashful.
Lowering my head, I looked at the wall.
Called to, a thousand times, I never looked back.

Fenollosa:

At fifteen I first opened my brows (i.e., first knew what
married life meant—now she opens her eyebrows, smooth-
ing out the wrinkles between her brows—awoke to the
meaning of love)
And so I desired to live and die with you—even after death
I wished to be with you, even as dust and even as ashes
[*word illegible*] together
I always had in me the faith of holding to pillars
And why should I think of climbing the husband looking
out terrace?

Pound:

At fifteen I stopped scowling,
I desired my dust to be mingled with yours
Forever and forever and forever.
Why should I climb the look out?

Fenollosa:

> At sixteen, however, you had to go far away
> Toward Shoku, passing through the difficult [*word illegible;*
>   straits?] of Yenyotai at Kuto (*transcription:* KU TO YEN
>   YO TAI; ku to = locality, yen yo = eddy?)
> In May not to be touched (five-months-not-must-touch)
> Monkeys cry sorrowful above heaven.

Pound:

> At sixteen you departed,
> You went into far Ku-to-yen, by the river of swirling eddies,
> And you have been gone five months.
> The monkeys make sorrowful noise overhead.

Fenollosa:

> Your footsteps made by your reluctant departure in front
>   of our gate
> One by one have been grown up with green moss
> These mosses have grown so deep that it is difficult to wipe
>   them away
> And the fallen leaves in [*word illegible*] autumn wind
> Which (to my thoughts only) appear to come earlier than
>   usual
> It being already August, the butterflies are yellow
> As yellow as they are, they fly in pairs on the Western
>   garden grass
> Affected at this (absence), my heart pains
> The longer absence lasts, the deeper I mourn my early time
>   [*word illegible;* paint?] face, will pass to oldness, to my
>   regret.
> If you will be coming down the three narrows sooner
>   or later (sooner (or)-later-descend-three-whirls; three
>   whirls = name of shoot on Yangtse Kiang)
> Please let me know by writing (beforehand-write-letter-
>   report-family-home)

For I will go out to meet you, not saying that the way is far
And will directly come to Chofusa.

Pound:

You dragged your feet when you went out.
By the gate now, the moss is grown, the different mosses,
Too deep to clear them away!
The leaves fall early this autumn, in wind.
The paired butterflies are already yellow with August
Over the grass in the West garden;
They hurt me. I grow older.
If you are coming down through the narrows of the river
    Kiang,
Please let me know beforehand,
And I will come out to meet you
                As far as Chofu-Sa.

Mrs. Pound recalled to me that at first Pound wanted to use the word *bangs* in the opening line. She declared this a "beastly Americanism"; in England, one said *fringes*. Pound found an excellent solution avoiding both words.

"At fourteen I married My Lord you" is an inspired stroke of translating; the phrase "My Lord you" resumes a whole society. And we see that the touching line "Forever and forever and forever," in which the girl's naive yearning comes to fullest expression, is Pound's creation. He justified such translator's liberties in writing of his own Cavalcanti renditions: "As to the atrocities of my translation, all that can be said in excuse is that they are, I hope, for the most part intentional, and committed with the aim of driving the reader's perception further into the original than it would without them have penetrated." And Pound has dropped two complete lines of the Fenollosa draft on the "general principle of not putting in mere words that occur in original when they contribute nothing to the SENSE of the translation" (letter to Glenn Hughes, 1927).

There is one downright mistake in Pound's final version —but does it matter? *Kiang* is rendered as a proper name; in fact, it means simply river. However, would *the Yangtse River* really have meant more to the nonspecialist reader? It would surely have been clumsier musically.

After editing the Fenollosa papers, Pound found himself drawn toward the Confucian ethical system that had enabled a steady accumulation and transmission of cultural goods for 2500 years. This finally led him to translate Confucius and the Confucian Odes and call himself a Confucian. He was especially pleased (Mrs. Pound told me) that Voltaire had ended his history of Louis XIV with a chapter on China; that was just where he himself would have ended it, Pound said. Pound fancied a direct influence of Chinese ideas on the eighteenth-century French rationalists and, through them, on the founders of the American republic. At Saint Elizabeth's he spoke of this more than once. And the similarities between the Chinese Neoconfucian outlook of the eighteenth century and the contemporary European Deist philosophy are indeed striking. We know that the French encyclopedists admired China and imagined that here was an ideal land of philosopher kings. The idea of an influence is intriguing.

Among the Fenollosa papers Pound found several versions of a lecture on the Chinese ideogram, and he blended them with miscellaneous Fenollosa notes to make "The Chinese Written Character as a Medium for Poetry," first published in *The Little Review* (September–December 1919). This brilliant essay says that the quintessential merit of Chinese characters is their nearness to the things they represent, since the characters are merely stylized pictures. "In reading Chinese we do not seem to be juggling mental counters, but to be watching *things* work out their fate," writes Fenollosa. *The Cantos* were themselves formed by the desire to cleave as close as possible to the things described, through direct, practical, purposeful language —and Fenollosa's essay may well have given *The Cantos* their aesthetic basis, as Hugh Kenner declares.

Fenollosa and Pound's "etymosinology" (Achilles Fang's neologism) has met a chilly reception among scholars of Chinese, who point out that only a small percentage of the ideograms have purely pictorial components. The characters began as pictures, to be sure, but in the combination of ideograms to produce new and more complex ideograms, one element of the new ideogram usually has a purely phonetic value. Many of Fenollosa and Pound's examples are dead wrong in their etymology, often because they ignore phonetic considerations. But is Fenollosa's thesis incorrect? I believe not. Fenollosa was showing what makes Chinese unique among languages. Though what he says is true to a lesser degree than he thought, that does not invalidate his general contention. He has accurately put his finger on the originality and genius of Chinese. Fenollosa and Pound give us a good reason for studying Chinese— which the professional sinologues do not.

Pound never went to the Far East, though he wrote several times in letters that he hoped to make the trip. The reason was plain lack of money. The unavailability of the relatively few dollars needed to get Pound to the East is really enough to make a wise man weep. The effects, on himself and on our common East-West civilization, would surely have been enormous.

He had no direct connection with the East after the Japanese painter Tami Koumé, who helped him with obscure points in the Fenollosa notes, died in the Tokyo earthquake of 1923. But then in 1937 the Japanese poet Kitasono Katue sent him a copy of *Vou*, a surrealist verse magazine published in Tokyo. Pound arranged for the publication of *Vou* poets in *The Townsman* and the *New Directions* anthology, and began a correspondence with Kitasono that lasted several decades, interrupted only by World War II. Pound never grasped how little Kitasono was interested in traditional Oriental things, and wrote him about the Noh and Confucius, assuming that these subjects fascinated Kitasono too. They did not; the gap between the old and the new is far greater in Japan than in the West. Kitasono told me he could understand the Noh in Pound's English but not in the old Japanese. When Omar Pound was in Japan, he and I asked Kitasono to accompany us to a Noh performance. He sent his wife instead, and she excused herself after watching the performance for a few minutes. The "new" Japanese find the Noh intolerably boring.

In June 1954, I visited Fenollosa's grave at the Miidera, a temple overlooking Lake Biwa near Kyoto. The poet Fujitomi Yasuo and I found the Miidera after wandering up and up through the great cryptomeria forest of the temple preserve—until we emerged, and saw the temple with its elegantly sloping roofs, like a bird ready to fly. Beneath, an immense vista of Lake Biwa, a great blue surrounded by mountains. Timeless! But not quite. Just under the temple was an American army camp. Luckily the mountain on which the Miidera stood was so steep that the camp was invisible.

Fenollosa lies in a clearing among the trees, Biwa gracefully beneath: a stone urn resting on a concrete base. Fujitomi and I stood awhile, perhaps thinking of the obscure destinies that had brought his notes to Pound's eye, and himself here. Then we returned to the Miidera, where a young attendant priest waited, friendly and very eager to please, his white robe marked with food stains. He showed us letters Mrs. Fenollosa had written the temple abbot from

Alabama during the nineteen-forties. In her old age, she had become a devotee of world religious brotherhood, or some such, and her letters were full of ungainly preachments. But many (even poets) become a bit fanatic as they age.

I described my visit in a letter to Pound, and he recorded it in the last line of his Canto 89:

> I want Frémont looking at mountains
> or, if you like, Reck, at Lake Biwa,

Frémont was of course the American explorer of the West; and I suppose that for Pound I was another such explorer. He may have seen in my visit to Fenollosa's grave that meeting of East and West which was his dream. With the next lines—the opening ones of Canto 90—the third and final section of *The Cantos* begins. In Pound's Paradiso, East and West are joined.

4

Ear for the Sea Surge

> And poor old Homer blind, blind as a bat
> Ear, ear for the sea surge. . . .
>   [Canto 2]

Only one thing is indispensable to a poet: EAR—a sense of sound. He can be brilliantly original, he can express profound feelings, he can show us wise and complex (or simple) attitudes to life, and all these are praiseworthy, but without an EAR, he is no poet. Pound has that EAR, more so than any other poet of his time.

By laying out *The Cantos* on such a vast scale unbounded by conventional poetic forms, Pound gave himself a gargantuan scope for variations in sound. The prosody of *The Cantos* is, in Pound's view, the sound itself. He wrote me a succinct definition in 1955: "Prosody: the articulation of the total sound of a poem, whether of 2 lines or 200 cantos."

EAR begins with skill in onomatopoeia, reproduction of natural sounds in verse. The lines from Canto 2 cited above refer to the Homeric sound qualities—what Andrew Lang called "The surge and thunder of the Odyssey"—and specifically to the oft-repeated phrase

para thina poluphloisboio thalassēs

176

("by the shore of the much-roaring sea"), which Pound called "magnificent onomatopoeia . . . the rush of the waves on the sea-beach and their recession." Canto 20 presents something similar, though here the sea sounds are more muted

> And the blue water dusky beneath them,
>> pouring there into the cataract,
> With noise of sea over shingle,
>> striking with:
>> hah hah ahah thmm, thunb, ah
>> woh woh araha thumm, bhaaa

In Canto 18 too we hear Pound's love of pure sound

> And the first thing Dave lit on when they got there
> Was a buzz-saw,
> And he put it through an ebony log: whhssh, t tttt,
> Two days' work in three minutes.

Onomatopoeia—the matching of sound to sense—is in fact the heart of *all* poetry. The verse magically assumes the qualities of the thing described; the texture of the words mirrors the subject. Hence Pound's interest in Chinese, where the ideogram often actually depicts the subject. And he admired Dante's acute sensitivity to word texture, when that poet classified his words as "buttered," "shaggy," "combed," and "hairy." "The science of the music of words and the knowledge of their magical powers has fallen away since men invoked Mithra by a sequence of pure vowel sounds," Pound declared in 1910. He set out to acquire that science.

Pound's command of rhythm is an exciting thing. I never fail to get a lift out of reading the lines from "Hugh Selwyn Mauberley" describing "Brennbaum the Impeccable":

The sky-like limpid eyes,
The circular infant's face,
The stiffness from spats to collar
Never relaxing into grace;

The first line has a driving, almost regular, iambic meter. In each successive line the meter becomes less regular, until in the fourth line there is only one strong syllable, the last. And this is a perfect match of sound to sense: the line is itself stiff, unnatural, until it finally relaxes with the closing word *grace*.

A similar virtuoso trick—for a different purpose—is found in "Exile's Letter," a poem from "Cathay":

The foreman of Kan Chu, drunk, danced
    because his long sleeves wouldn't keep still
With that music playing,

In the second line here, the restlessness of the ever-swinging sleeves of the Chinese robe is evoked by the rhythm: every syllable of the line is strong except for the first syllable of "because" and the second of "wouldn't." With *still*, the last strong syllable, the line itself finally becomes still. Word music can hardly be carried farther.

The music of words—sounds and rhythms—was always Pound's primary concern. At Saint Elizabeth's I asked him how he pronounced Provençal. "Just try to get a good sound out of it," Pound said. He wrote: "Poetry withers and 'dries out' when it leaves music, or at least an imagined music, too far behind it. . . . Poetry must be read as music and not as oratory." For Pound rhythm, or cadence, is the means of emotional expression—"the perception of the intellect is given in the word, that of the emotions in the cadence," he writes. It even determines the poem's form (instead of vice versa): "Any given rhythm implies about it a complete musical form"—a theory he carries out, on a vast scale, in *The Cantos*.

That poem is a gigantic exercise in word music. All kinds of musical variation are found in it, and as it moves toward its Paradiso section, the verbal texture becomes that of cut stone: the words are chipped, hard, durable. And in fact Pound has described verse writing as "cutting a shape in time."

An important reason for this verbal texture, where each word has a sharp hewed-stone cutting edge, is accuracy of language. There is no verbal flabbiness; the words follow precisely the thing described. Pound expresses himself directly, avoids figurative language. A turning point for Pound may have been the incident described in William Carlos Williams' *Kora in Hell:*

> My parent had been holding forth in downright sentences upon my own "idle nonsense" when he turned and became equally vehement concerning something Ezra had written: what in heaven's name Ezra meant by "jewels" in a verse that had come between them. These jewels—rubies, sapphires, amethysts and what not, Pound went on to explain with great determination and care, were the backs of books as they stood on a man's shelf. "But why in heaven's name don't you say so then?" was my father's triumphant and crushing rejoinder.

Concerning which, Pound wrote Williams in 1920: "Your old man was certainly dead right. And whatever t'ell I said ten years ago, I certainly have since then endeavoured 'to why in the hell or heaven' *say it* and NOT summat else."

With hammering repetition, Pound's criticism demands precision of statement, particularization, "efficient writing —even in verse." The medieval scholastic philosophers' care for terminology pleased him. When this care is exercised, he thought, words are not prized for words' sake, but for their congruence to the matter described. Pound admired Stendhal for, he said, fixing attention on things rather than words.

He attacked bad writing—"fogged language," generalized, hazy expression—as a doctor attacks germs. "The man of understanding can no more sit quiet and resigned while his country lets its literature decay, and lets good writing meet with contempt, than a good doctor could sit quiet and contented while some ignorant child was infecting itself with tuberculosis under the impression that it was merely eating jam tarts," Pound declared in the *ABC of Reading*. Curiously enough—because he seemed at the opposite pole from Pound in political ideas—Bertold Brecht used the same simile, comparing himself to a doctor who chooses to treat a young prostitute (the East German government) rather than an old roué (the West German). Both Pound and Brecht had a stringently moral view of their art.

Pound makes use of an enormous vocabulary, not for parade or show, but because he wants precise language. The words are applied with dead-eye accuracy and naturalness, so that we usually feel *this* is the *mot juste*, no other word is possible. Pound probably has *more* words than any English-language poet since Browning. And like Joyce and Thomas Mann, he occasionally shows his virtuosity by inventing archaic language that sounds authentic. But most of all his linguistic genius is found in his command of real speech.

I remember sitting across from Robert Frost at a Cambridge, Massachusetts, tea party (or cocktail party?) in honor of a visiting Japanese novelist. The novelist spoke no English, Frost no Japanese. For a while I tried interpreting, but gave it up when a Japanese appeared who knew both tongues far better than I did. Old Frost squinted across at me and said, "Y'know, learnin' a lotta languages don't really help a poet in his work. What counts is an ear for your own language, for real speech."

And I—a poet who have studied some of ten languages —could hardly agree more.

5

The Elusive Mr. Pound

After we have dipped deep in the *Personae* and that magical poem *The Cantos*, with its dazzling array of characters stretching through all history, we may be astonished by Pound's virtuoso ability to make people come alive by speaking with their voices—and we may be a bit lost. Where is the poet behind all this? We may learn who all his characters are. But who is Mr. Pound?

The elusive Ezra Pound certainly does not lay his soul bare, in the manner of the romantic poets. He believes that outward, objective things make the poem—being thus, as Donald Davie has pointed out, at the opposite pole from the Symbolists, for whom the poem is an "objective correlative" of an inner experience. Pound's feelings—the subjective, personal element—only impinge upon the poem laterally, coloring the description and influencing the choice of things described. Or at least that is Pound's intention.

It might be objected that *The Cantos* are full of personal outbursts too; much of that poem is highly personal. I want to suggest that Pound had to deal with some severe internal struggles, one of which was expressed in the famed lines from *The Pisan Cantos*, "Pull down thy vanity!" Marianne Moore had written, in the poem of hers that was Pound's favorite: "There never was a war that was not inward." Pound was struggling with himself for objectivity.

His ego was naturally enormous. No one without a well-developed ego could have undertaken the dry-cleaning of English letters and carried through the leviathanic *Cantos*. E. E. Cummings once noted he had never once observed a single peripherally situated ego; therefore he cheerfully wrote most of his poetry from a highly personal stand-point. But Pound was trying to grow out of a subjective generation which cultivated an inarticulate *Schwärmerei*. Like the Buddha's followers, he realized that the ego is the great hindrance to perception. So he tried to discipline his "I" by making it an "eye," and chose the form of the *persona*—or mask—in which to cast much of his poetry.

His model for the *personae* was the pungent "dramatic monologue" of Browning—"Old Hippety-Hop o' the ac-cents," Pound addressed him affectionately. Browning used the form as merely a dramatic device. With Pound, on the other hand, the *persona* can be so deeply felt that it threatens to become a mystical belief. He states the matter quite plainly in a very early poem, "Histrion":

> No man hath dared to write this thing as yet,
> And yet I know, how that the souls of all men great
> At times pass through us,
> And we are melted into them, and are not
> Save reflections of their souls.
> Thus I am Dante for a space and am
> One François Villon, Ballad-Lord, and thief
> Or am such holy ones I may not write
> Lest blasphemy be writ against my name,
> This for an instant and the flame be gone.

*   *   *

> So cease we from all being for the time
> And these, the Masters of the soul, live on.

The *persona* can also be a form of self-discovery for Pound, as the most famous of them, Hugh Selwyn Mauberley. The problem of Mauberley's identity has occupied several critics. Hugh Kenner calls Mauberley Pound's antithesis, a character with whom Pound is anxious not to be confused; Donald Davie, however, points out that Mauberley is very like Pound himself. And when we note that the first section of the poem is entitled "E.P. Ode pour l'election de son sepulchre," we are too tempted to conclude that the "he" of the poem is Pound. But Pound has himself answered the question here: "Of course I'm no more Mauberley than Eliot is Prufrock," he wrote Felix Schelling (and he said the same when I asked him).

Mauberley is just another stage character, a *persona*. Pound's idea of the *persona* derives from the stage—the word means the mask worn by Roman actors, or the role itself—and in the *persona* Mauberley we have an irony that underlies many stage effects: the author and audience know something about the performer that he himself does not know. The audience is allowed to smile at the performer's vanity or foolishness. In "Mauberley" the play is certainly autobiographical, but it remains a stage play. Here Pound uses the form to satirize himself, exaggerating the weaknesses of Pound the aesthete. He had already decided that his own work must become more robust. Hence *The Cantos*—and in "Mauberley" we see why.

Pound was surely a man of many inner struggles (we all are, but Pound had more within him to keep in order). The result is sometimes chaos—he once characterized his own talk as "an explosion in an art museum"—and the first visual impression of many of *The Cantos* is that somehow the lines have become jumbled. The struggles within

Pound caused him to mar some of his finest things—for example, the magnificent Chinese Cantos, which open with an ugly diatribe against usury. Yet order—objective depersonal order—was Pound's ideal, and *The Cantos* are full of his longing for it. The man who exalts the homestead in *The Cantos* had himself never owned a piece of land. Pound was essentially so protean, vivacious, volatile, that perhaps the only place where he could find the order he needed was in the patterned changefulness of nature.

The great process of nature, as seen by the Chinese Neoconfucian philosophers, became central to Pound's outlook, and the idea of following nature shaped *The Cantos*. In the *Paris Review* interview, he says of *The Cantos*: "Only a musical form would take the material, and the Confucian universe as I see it is a universe of interacting strains and tensions." Pound conceives of the cosmos as dynamic, a *process*—so the Cantos *flow*. They "move like the wind," as Mozart said of his own music. Pound, the archhater of smugness, constantly jars the reader by quick changes: Ovidian metamorphoses, leaps from one time in history to another.

What Pound calls "the process" of nature is the Chinese *tao*, usually rendered "the way." The Neoconfucians explained all nature as the interaction of passive and active principles, which together form a harmonious "process." Nature is a harmony, the standard for measuring all men's actions. Nature is good; men must cleave to it.

Thus Herakles says in Pound's rendition of Sophocles' *Trachiniae:*

> SPLENDOUR,
>   IT ALL COHERES

which is, Pound writes, "the key phrase, for which the play exists." We find it echoed, and glossed, in Canto 116:

> i.e. it coheres all right
>> even if my notes do not cohere

"It" is nature. This is the culmination of Pound's wisdom. Nature's process is a great coherence. We must follow it. The external world is all.

Beneath the practical hard-boiled man of facts, Pound is a mystic—and this becomes most evident in the last few Cantos. Egoism has been burned away. The poet is finally OU TIS, no man (Odysseus' answer to the Cyclops), as he had written earlier:

> For the seven lakes, and by no man these verses
>
> *   *   *
>
> OU TIS, OU TIS? Odysseus
>> the name of my family.

The evasive Odysseus is Pound's prototype. Like Odysseus, Pound is a wanderer who seeks the way home. For Pound, the way is wisdom, home is the truth. In this quest he must be like the Ithacan: *polutropos*—shifty, supple, protean. He is not to be caught in any formula. Where, then, is the elusive Mr. Pound? With Whitman, he might say: "look for me under your boot-soles."

6

Reading the Cantos

A dear friend of mine, rather given to bombast and over-statement, once declared "Everything Pound has written is *sacred* to me." I was a bit taken aback, and asked if he wouldn't care to qualify that statement *at all*. "Well, I haven't read *The Cantos*," he admitted.

It turned out that my friend's opinion was based on the *Personae*, while he considered *The Cantos* impossible to read. As a severe Latinophile and teacher of Latin, he had every right to admire the *Personae*, for many of these are—to paraphrase a remark of Ford Madox Ford—the best Latin poems in the English language. And there is no doubt that *The Cantos* are difficult, often more difficult than they should be (which Pound himself admitted in the *Paris Review* interview). But one should not, therefore, summarily dismiss this extraordinarily beautiful and rewarding poem.

Life magazine calls *The Cantos* "turgid" (in a 1964 article on Pound). Nothing could be less true. There is nothing pompous or inflated about Pound's style, which in fact is of a crystalline clarity and precision. What gives difficulty is the range of reference. Pound's poem has an enormous scope, and he does not care to load it down with identification of his references. "Where are we?" he writes at the beginning of Canto 21. The reader often wonders too.

The best way of approaching *The Cantos* is simply to stride right through the poem, letting the words fall on your ear, keeping calm and self-possessed even when arrantly obscure names and quotations appear on the way. Your purpose is to enjoy the sound, and pick up what beauty and entertainment you can. This first hike might be lively enough to make you want to learn more about what is happening. You next turn to *Literary Essays of Ezra Pound* or *Guide to Kulchur* or *The Letters of Ezra Pound*, all of which are in themselves rewarding enough to read. Then back to *The Cantos*, as you are presumably by now a bit further into Pound's world. This time more light will probably appear. If needed, the *Annotated Index to the Cantos of Ezra Pound* by John H. Edwards and William W. Vasse (University of California Press, 1959), while not absolutely reliable, will help clarify obscure points. But looking up every reference is a dull business, probably not recommendable until you are at an advanced stage of reading *The Cantos*. Better let the poem sing to you.

One point that must be emphasized is that the poem means precisely what it says. The reader must not suspect that one thing stands for another. There are no symbols. The things presented are regarded as in themselves significant. Nevertheless, the poem is not formless. Pound is intensely concerned with the relations between things, "The *forma*, the immortal *concetto*, the concept, the dynamic form which is like the rose-pattern driven into the dead iron filings by the magnet."

Pound leaps from thing to thing not out of whimsy, but because he wants to show relations between things that only appear to be disparate. His interests are vast, and he is constantly tying together different bits of these interests, indicating connections. Ronald Duncan has pointed out that in this sense Pound is deeply religious, as the word *religio* means "to connect." Pound once remarked: "People quite often think me crazy when I make a jump instead of a step, just as if all jumps were unsound and never carried one anywhere." Pound's unmethodical method in fact derives from a very rational dislike of systematization, a habit which this century has carried to the point of mania.

The Cantos are ordered according to what Pound calls "the ideogrammatic method." This is the method of juxtaposition followed by the Chinese in creating new and compound ideograms. Two or more ideograms are put together to make a new ideogram; understood as a whole, they create a new meaning. This also is often the method of Chinese poetry. Seemingly disparate objects are described seriatim. They are felt to modify one another and, perceived together, they express a sentiment, a mood, or an atmosphere. The whole is greater than the parts. Probably because of Pound's influence on him, Eliot used the "ideogrammatic method" in *The Waste Land* and, notably, in *Rhapsody on a Windy Night*.

"Great bulk, huge mass, thesaurus," begins Canto 5—and this we can take as describing all *The Cantos*. Pound has spread his net wide; he wants to tell "the tale of the tribe," to "give the true meaning of history as one man has found it." Epics have always done this, but now cultures are coalescing, communications are much quicker, and our history is the whole world's. "When it comes to the question of poetry, a great many people don't want to know that their own country does not occupy ALL the available surface of the planet," Pound complained.

Hence we find a good dozen languages represented in *The Cantos*. To the criticism that the reader cannot be expected to know so many languages, Pound said at Saint Elizabeth's, in effect: "I can't deny that these languages *exist*. They are there. I only put them in the poem." He wrote Hubert Creekmore:

> I believe that when finished, *all* foreign words in the Cantos, Greek, etc., will be underlinings, not necessary to the sense, in one way. I mean a complete sense will exist without them; it will be there in the American text, but the Greek, ideograms, etc., will indicate a *duration* from where or since when. If you can find any *briefer* means of getting this repeat or resonance, tell papa, and I will try to employ it.

That is, the foreign quotations are there to increase *The Cantos'* time and space scale. And Pound adds:

> ALL typographic disposition, placings of words *on* the page, is intended to facilitate the reader's intonation, whether he be reading silently to self or aloud to friends. Given time and technique I might even put down the musical notation of passages or "breaks into song."
>
> There is *no intentional* obscurity. There is condensation to maximum attainable. It is impossible to make the deep as quickly comprehensible as the shallow.

It might be added, in Pound's defense that there *are* things which can be said in one language and not in another. The Chinese ideograms really cannot be translated; Greek, Latin, Provençal, French have their own idioms and music unrenderable in English. Pound often uses words in foreign tongues because he is fascinated with the sound.

Pound admired the Japanese Noh drama program—a one-day series of plays—because, he said, it gave "a complete diagram of life." His intuition that literature should set forth a whole view of the world, in this century of skepti-

cism and intellectual fragmentation, found expression in
The Cantos. Like the *Divine Comedy*, *The Cantos* intend
to show good and evil—Hell, Purgatory, and Paradise—
and they very roughly correspond to Dante's three-part
organization. The first Canto describes a descent to Hell
(Odysseus'); Cantos 14, 15, and the beginning of 16 depict
a Hell; the publisher's blurb to the *Rock Drill* section
(whose style bears traces of having been written by
Pound) says that with Canto 90 *The Cantos* "move into
their third and final phase: the 'domination of benevolence.'" However, it is difficult to see where Pound's Inferno shades off into a Purgatorio.

In his *Paris Review* interview, the poet offered some
very interesting illumination of the question of *The Cantos'*
organization:

> I was not following the three divisions of the *Divine
> Comedy* exactly. One can't follow the Dantesquan cos-
> mos in an age of experiment. But I have made the divi-
> sion between people dominated by emotion, people
> struggling upwards, and those who have some part of
> the divine vision. The thrones in Dante's *Paradiso* are
> for the spirits of the people who have been responsible
> for good government. The thrones in the *Cantos* are an
> attempt to move out from egoism and to establish some
> definition of an order possible or at any rate conceiv-
> able on earth.

But he admitted: "It is difficult to write a paradiso when all
the superficial indications are that you ought to write an
apocalypse. It is obviously much easier to find inhabitants
for an inferno or even a purgatorio." Pound recognized
that Dante's mathematically exact organization was not
suited to the more complex twentieth century. He wrote
R. P. Blackmur: "And we agree, je crois, that one can no
longer put Mt. Purgatory forty miles high in the midst of
Australian sheep land."

Already in *The Spirit of Romance*, published 1910, Pound expresses the view of time that is basic to *The Cantos:* "It is dawn at Jerusalem while midnight hovers above the Pillars of Hercules. All ages are contemporaneous." This idea that all time is eternally present seems to have strongly influenced T. S. Eliot, for the structure of *The Waste Land* is founded on it, and the concept appears also in the *Four Quartets. The Cantos* bring all history before us, live and of this moment—one of their brilliant achievements. A trick to achieve immediacy is Pound's repeated use of the first-person pronoun. The poet takes on the masks of a variety of historical personages and *becomes* these people. The effect is to make the past astonishingly alive, and the poem achieves an epic scope in its wide sweep of time.

Among the speculations of his booklet *A Packet for Ezra Pound*, William Butler Yeats described *The Cantos* as a fugue. At Saint Elizabeth's Pound declared that Yeats' essay had done more than anything to create confusion about *The Cantos*, and suggested that he had followed, rather, "the ideogrammatic method" in composing the poem. It is hard to say why Pound was so violently against Yeats' idea that *The Cantos* are a fugue (which, Yeats wrote, was how Pound himself expressed it, at Rapallo in 1929). He may have felt that Yeats' view suggested a formal over-all organization, implying that the formal aspects were more important than the poem's content. But I am not sure that we can abandon the analogy to music. In addition to the fact that every line of *The Cantos* is interesting for its rhythm and verbal melody, the whole structure has a musicality. As in music, themes appear and are repeated. There are variations on these themes, which please because they meet or deceive our expectations. Many individual phrases and verse lines, melodic and moving in themselves, return again and again, as a horn may suddenly resound amid the strings in an orchestra. Whatever the cause, *The Cantos* do sound good, very good, when heard. Mrs. Pound told me she always advises people to approach *The Cantos* by reading them aloud.

And that seems to me the wisest way.

INDEX

INDEX

Abercrombie, Lascelles, 15
Adams, Brooks, 58, 61
Adams, Henry, 79
Adams, John, 51
Aiken, Conrad, 28, 87
Aldington, Richard, 13, 19, 23–24, 26, 30–31, 34, 39, 142, 163
Allen, Robert L., 65
Anderson, Margaret, 39
Andrewes, Lancelot, 80
Antheil, George, 46, 93
Aragon, Louis, 40
Arnold, Thurman, 133
Atlantic Monthly, The, 163
Auden, W. H., 71–72

Barry, Iris, 32–33
Beach, Sylvia, 40–41, 43
Beerbohm, Sir Max, 6, 49
Bentley, Eric, 128–129
Binyon, Lawrence, 54
Bird, William, 41

Bishop, Elizabeth, 87
Black Mountain group, 107
Blackmur, R. P., 191
Blunt, Wilfred Scawen, 27
Bollingen Prize, 90
Brancusi, 40, 42
Bridson, D. G., 81
Browning, Robert, 10, 118, 180, 183
Brunnenburg, 6, 139–141, 144–146, 166
Bunting, Basil, 51–52, 55, 102, 109, 127
Burdick, Representative Usher L., 66, 130

Cann, Louise Gebhard, 49, 110
Cantos, The, 7, 28, 33–35, 39, 45–47, 49–50, 52, 63–64, 79, 87, 89, 94–96, 101, 113–117, 119–125, 128–129, 139–141, 144, 147, 150,

153–155, 160, 161, 164–165,
172–173, 175–179, 182–193
Pisan, 11–12, 16, 18, 27, 43, 62,
   64–65, 78, 90, 92, 104, 106,
   115, 120, 123, 125, 140, 154,
   183
Carruth, Hayden, 90–91
Catullus, Gaius Valerius, 21, 43,
   161
Cavalcanti, Guido, 17, 49, 93, 99
Chicago, 18, 156
China, 18, 26, 50, 99, 153, 155, 172
Chute, Desmond, 5, 49
Cleaves, Francis, 119
Cocteau, Jean, 40
Confucius, 49, 52, 58, 60, 64, 89,
   94, 101, 102, 105–106, 116, 129,
   134, 162, 172, 174
Coolidge, Calvin, 36
Cornell, Julian, 67
Cory, Daniel, 150
Cournos, John, 28
Cowley, Malcolm, 165
Creekmore, Hubert, 190
Cummings, E. E., 46, 58, 68, 82,
   86–87, 91–92, 101, 114, 130, 142,
   164, 183

Daniel, Arnaut, 44, 161
Dante, 10, 17, 28, 33, 37, 44, 113,
   131, 143, 165, 177, 183, 191
   Divine Comedy, 33, 54, 165,
   191
Davenport, Guy, 95
Davie, Donald, 182, 184
Dial, The, 46

Dolmetsch, Arnold, 93
Doolittle, Hilda (H. D.), 8–10,
   19–20, 23, 24, 29
Douglas, C. H., 34, 42, 44
Duncan, Ronald, 99, 189

Egoist, The, 30–32, 34, 45, 80
Egoist Press, 37
Eliot, Thomas Stearns, 14, 23, 25,
   27–31, 36, 43–45, 51, 58, 79–
   83, 87, 93, 102–103, 112, 114,
   119, 129–130, 140, 142, 143, 163,
   164, 166, 184, 189, 192
   *Love Song of J. Alfred Pruf-
   rock*, 28–29, 164, 184
   The Waste Land, 43–45, 164,
   189, 192
English Review, The, 15
Epoca, 141–142
Epstein, Jacob, 16, 28, 93
Exile, The, 49, 51

Faber and Faber, 102, 142
Fang, Achilles, 106, 119, 162, 173
Fenollosa, Ernest, 21–22, 119,
   166–175
Fitts, Dudley, 53
Fjelde, Rolf, 41, 92, 106, 107
Flaubert, Gustave, 40
Fleming, Rudd, 105–106
Fletcher, John Gould, 25
Flint, F. S., 17, 23
Ford, Ford Madox (*see* Hueffer,
   Ford Madox)
Fox, D. C., 99

Frankfurter, Felix, 128
Freud, Sigmund, 6, 80
Froebenius, Leo, 49–50, 99, 116,
 118, 153
 Institute, 104
Frost, Robert, 20, 29, 133, 155,
 180–181

Gaudier-Brzeska, Henri, 32, 34,
 93, 123, 139, 147
Georgians, 14–16
Ginsberg, Allen, 87
Giovannini, Giovanni, 66
Gonne, Maude, 35–36
Gosse, Edmund, 163
Gourmont, Remy de, 157
Graves, Robert, 68
Gregory, Lady, 12, 23
Guthrie, Ramon, 42

Hailey, Idaho, 3, 5, 143
Hall, Donald, 141, 155, 165
Hamilton, Edith, 88–89
Hamilton College, 7, 56, 109
Heine, Heinrich, 116, 118
Hemingway, Ernest, 15, 27, 41–
 42, 44, 51, 64, 81–84, 103, 130,
 147
 L'Herne, 53, 143
Heyman, Katherine Ruth, 10
Hightower, James Robert, 119
Hitler, Adolph, 55, 57, 116, 123,
 125, 127–128
Horace, 21

Horton, David, 86, 102, 105, 113,
 134–135
Housman, A. E., 158–159
Howe, Quincy, Jr., 101
Hueffer, Ford Madox, 15–16, 28,
 34, 37, 39, 40, 157, 165, 166, 187
Hughes, Langston, 87
Hulme, T. E., 16–18, 34, 99, 100,
 123, 164
 Speculations, 17, 99
Hutchins, Patricia, 29–30

i, 101
Ibbotson, J. D., 7
Imagism, 9, 23–26, 30
Indiscretions, 4–5
Ito, Michio, 96–97

James, Henry, 37, 58, 130, 155
Japan, 17, 21, 25, 89, 96–101, 108,
 109, 148, 153, 166–175
Jefferson, Thomas, 51–52
Jepson, Edgar, 163
Jiménez, Juan Ramón, 84, 95–96,
 122
Jiménez, Zenobia, 84, 95, 122
Joyce, James, 31–32, 36, 42–43,
 51, 58, 81, 130, 180
 Ulysses, 32, 36, 42–43, 81
Jung, Carl, 80

Kaltenborn, H. V., 56, 57
Kasper, John, 103–104

Katue, Kitasono, 17, 97–98, 100, 101, 159, 173–174
Keats, John, 15, 119
Kenner, Hugh, 111, 173, 184
Kensington, 23, 28–30, 142
Kerouac, Jack, 87
Koumé, Tami, 173

La Driere, J. C., 105
Laughlin, James, 52, 67, 68
Lampman, Rex, 103
Leavis, F. R., 160
Lekakis, Michael, 108, 145
Lewis, Wyndham, 20, 26, 27, 32–34, 36, 51, 109, 114, 116, 123, 147, 157, 163
Little Review, The, 36–37, 172
Liveright, Horace, 42
Longfellow, Henry Wadsworth, 4
Lorenzatos, Zesimos, 154–155
Lowell, Amy, 25, 156
Lowell, Robert, 87, 115

MacGregor, Robert, 135
MacLeish, Archibald, 7, 58, 67–68, 83, 88, 125–126, 129, 156
McPherson, Douglas, 93
Malatesta, Sigismundo, 52
Marsden, Dora, 30
Mathews, Elkin, 12–13, 18
Mauberley, Hugh Selwyn, 34, 38–39, 49, 123, 160, 161, 164, 177–178, 184
Mencken, H. L., 82–83, 87–88, 156

Monroe, Harriet, 15, 18–20, 22, 28, 29, 36, 49, 162
Moore, Frank Ledlie, 107–108, 114, 145–146
Moore, Marianne, 37, 58, 87, 122, 162, 183
Mullins, Eustace, 102–103, 114, 128, 150
Münch, Gerhart, 54
Munro, Harold, 32
Mussolini, Benito, 4, 54–55, 57, 59, 62, 112–113, 122–125, 157

New Age, The, 34, 93
New Directions, 53, 99, 135, 174
New Technics, 100
New Freewoman, The, 20, 30
Nobel Prize, 19, 84, 96
Noh, 22–23, 96, 154, 167, 174, 190
Norman, Charles, 46

Olson, Charles, 87, 107
Orage, A. W., 34

Paige, Douglass, 64, 82–83, 130
Paris Review, 117, 141, 165, 185, 187, 191
Pearson, Norman Holmes, 106, 135
Pennsylvania, University of, 7–8, 110
Personae, 12–13, 16, 18, 32, 49, 94, 101, 110, 113, 116, 160, 166, 182, 187

Petrarch, Francesco, 17

Philadelphia, 3, 5–6, 28, 39, 156

Poetry, 18–19, 21–25, 28–29, 32, 33, 45, 90–91

Poetry and Drama, 32

Poetry New York, 106–107

Pound, Dorothy Shakespear, devotion to Ezra Pound, 85–86

wife of Ezra Pound, 5–6, 11–13, 15, 22, 27, 29–31, 35, 40–42, 48–49, 52, 59, 63, 65, 71, 76, 84, 88, 94, 108, 110, 121, 123, 134, 135, 139–140, 145–147, 157, 171–172, 192

Americanism, 45, 51, 116–117, 155–159

character, 6–7, 42, 110–111

Pound, Ezra, childhood, 3–6

committed to Saint Elizabeth's Hospital, 70–71

declared insane, 68–72

disenchantment with England, 39, 48

diversity of interests, 31–32, 93

education, 3, 7–8

family, 3–6

feeling toward Jews, 28, 55, 58–59, 86–87, 116, 127–129, 131

first trip abroad, 6

helping other writers, 19–20, 24, 31–33, 36–37, 41–43, 45, 51, 54, 95–96

illness, 141–143

imprisonment, 63–70, 130

influence on literature, 71–72, 87, 101–102, 106, 153, 164, 192

and London, 3, 11–39

marriage, 27

and music, 46, 54, 93, 107–108, 120–121

in Paris, 40–47

as poet, 119–120, 130

politics, 4, 34, 54–56, 113, 115, 122–129, 154, 157, 180

poverty, 35, 42, 49, 54, 57–59, 69, 124

writers who influenced, 21–23, 51, 118, 164, 183

Pound, Homer, father of Ezra Pound, 5, 52

Pound, Isabel Weston, mother of Ezra Pound, 4, 6, 52

Pound, Mary, daughter of Ezra Pound, 62–63, 139–140

Pound, Omar, son of Ezra Pound, 102, 108–109, 118, 122, 132, 134, 174

Pound, Thaddeus Coleman, grandfather of Ezra Pound, 3–4

Propertius, Sextus, 21, 39, 163

Homage to Sextus Propertius, 38, 72, 160–163

Provence, 27–28

Quinn, John, 30, 33, 35, 44

Rachewiltz, Prince Boris de, son-in-law of Ezra Pound, 139–140

Rapallo, 5–6, 48–55, 63, 80, 82, 93, 95, 99, 124, 141, 143–144, 192

Read, Herbert, 17
Roosevelt, Franklin Delano, 58, 88, 115, 130, 132, 133
Rouse, W. H. D., 39, 54
Rudge, Olga, 54, 63, 102, 141–143, 148–150
    daughter Mary, 148

Saint Elizabeth's Hospital, 9–10, 15, 16, 20, 22, 37, 40–41, 52, 53, 65, 67
    description of, 75–77
    Ezra Pound's sentencing to, 70–71
    life at, 78–131, 156
    release from, 132–135
Santayana, George, 79, 115, 150
Saturday Review of Literature, The, 90
Schelling, Felix, 161, 184
Scriabin, Alexander, 10
Sette, 101
Sewanee Review, 143
Shakespear, Olivia, 11, 27, 109
Shakespeare and Company, 40–41
Shaw, Bernard, 43
Shuzo, Iwamoto, 97
Simpson, Dallam, 102
Social Credit, 34–35, 42, 44, 51, 53, 76, 86, 114, 123, 125
Stein, Gertrude, 40
Stendhal, 40, 180
Swabey, Henry, 80
Swinburne, Algernon Charles, 15, 163

Tagore, Rabindranath, 19, 153
Tate, Allen, 87
Taupin, René, 118
Tei, Miki, 97
Thompson, Virgil, 46
Three Mountains Press, 41
Townsman, The, 99, 174
T. P.'s Weekly, 24
transatlantic review, 40
Tura, Cosimo, 52

Untermeyer, Louis, 19

Vasse, Jack, 97
Vega, de, Lope, 9
Venice, 6, 10, 141, 143, 147–150
Villon, François, 40, 46, 116, 143, 183
Vorticism, 26, 28
Vou, 97–100, 173–174

Wabash College, 9
Wallace, Lew, 9
Weaver, Harriet, 30, 32, 43, 81
Whitman, Walt, 117, 186
Wilde, Oscar, 14, 21
Williams, William Carlos, 7–11, 39, 45, 51, 87, 92, 93, 107, 110, 135, 142, 163, 164, 179
Woburn Buildings, 11
Wordsworth, William, 15
World War I, 9, 26, 34–35, 93, 98, 122–123
Wyncote, Pennsylvania, 5, 18

Yale Poetry Review, The, 106, 120

Yasuo, Fujitomi, 101, 174

Yeats, John Butler, 18

Yeats, William Butler, 10–12, 15–16, 19, 21–23, 27, 31, 33, 35–36, 48, 49, 52, 87, 96, 103, 105, 114, 130, 164, 192

Zukofsky, Louis, 51, 55, 59, 79–80, 127, 128

ABOUT THE AUTHOR

MICHAEL RECK, fresh out of Harvard, went to visit Ezra Pound at Saint Elizabeth's Hospital in Washington, D.C., in 1951. Pound saw some promise in Reck's own poetry and enrolled him in the "Ezuversity," as Pound jocularly called his attempts to educate the young—even at that time Pound was still a tireless and selfless teacher. Over the next fifteen years Reck had a unique chance to observe this vigorous, brilliant, cantankerous, magnanimous poet, one of the central figures in this century's literature.

After taking an M.A. in Far Eastern languages at Harvard, Michael Reck worked for four years in publishing in New York. He then taught English, Greek, and Japanese at the University of Puerto Rico, and went to continue his studies in Germany, where he now lives on the Amersee near Munich. His poetry has been published in a number of magazines and in James Laughlin's *New Directions* anthology.